P9-CRJ-230

FREEWHEELING:
the Bicycle
Camping Book

FREEWHEELING:
the Bicycle
Camping
Book

RAYMOND BRIDGE

Stackpole Books

FREEWHEELING: THE BICYCLE CAMPING BOOK

Copyright © 1974 by
The Stackpole Company

Published by
STACKPOLE BOOKS
Cameron and Kelker Streets
Harrisburg, Pa. 17105

All rights reserved, including the right to reproduce this book or portions
thereof in any form or by any means, electronic or mechanical, including
photocopying, recording, or by any information storage and retrieval
system, without permission in writing from the publisher. All inquiries
should be addressed to Stackpole Books, Cameron and Kelker Streets,
Harrisburg, Pennsylvania 17105.

Printed in the U.S.A.

Library of Congress Cataloging in Publication Data

Bridge, Raymond.
    Freewheeling: the bicycle camping book.

    Bibliography: p.
    1. Cycling. 2. Camping. I. Title.
GV1041.B74   796.6   73-18255
ISBN 0-8117-2020-9

Dedicated to my mother,
who taught me to ride my 20-inch Huffy.

Other books by Raymond Bridge

THE COMPLETE SNOW CAMPER'S GUIDE
AMERICA'S BACKPACKING BOOK

Contents

INTRODUCTION   **9**

CHAPTER 1: WHAT IT'S ALL ABOUT   13

The joys of bicycling. Styles of touring. Travelling from
hostel to hotel, European style. Bicycle camping, carrying shelter and supplies along. Bicycle camping and
other sorts of self-propelled travel. Getting started.

CHAPTER 2: CAMPING ALONG THE ROAD   22

Cycle camping as an art in itself. Camping basics.
Choosing a site. Shelters. Cooking. Fires and stoves.
Lunches. Water. Clothing. Sleeping comfortably.
Flashlights and other accessories. Insects.

CHAPTER 3: SLEEPING BAGS AND TENTS   62

Choosing the expensive items of camping equipment.

CHAPTER 4: SPECIAL CAMPING SITUATIONS   **81**

Mountains. Cold weather. Deserts. Wet conditions.

CHAPTER 5: THE TOURING BICYCLE   **86**

The best type of cycle. Looking at a bicycle critically. Getting the right size. Gears and ratios. Tires. Cranks, pedals, hubs, wheels, and bottom brackets. Brakes. Seats and handlebars. Accessories. Repairs and maintenance. Transporting the bike.

CHAPTER 6: LOADING THE BIKE   **128**

Basic rules. Carriers. Packs. Making panniers and handlebar packs. Carrying children. Trailers.

CHAPTER 7: THE ART OF RIDING   **145**

Pace, rhythm, and cadence. Position and pedalling. Hills. Traffic. Special problems of riding with a load. Working with nature.

CHAPTER 8: SPECIAL RIDING CONDITIONS   **157**

Rain. Mountains. Cold weather, ice, and snow. Desert. Dirt and gravel roads. Night riding.

CHAPTER 9: PLANNING BICYCLE CAMPING TOURS   **168**

Checking the area. Roads. Daily itinerary. Finding the way. Equipment and provisions. Campgrounds. Saving money. Suggestions.

APPENDICES

    I   **Additional Reading**   **180**

    II   **Where To Get It**   **183**

    III   **Organizations**   **187**

       INDEX   **189**

Introduction

The lure of the open road! It was a romantic notion that lured most of us as kids, with thoughts of flowering fields, rugged mountain passes, the songs of birds, and the wind whipping through our hair. Alas, the modern automobile and superhighway have changed all that, and talk of the open road is more likely to evoke thoughts of nerve-racking daily commuting along clogged asphalt, through clouds of exhaust fumes. Even weekend drives or vacation trips rarely allow much joy to be extracted from driving along the road. One is always going either too slowly or too rapidly; the noise of the engine and soundproofing of the passenger compartment prevent one from telling whether the birds are singing or not, and losing oneself in the scenery is likely to be suicidal.

Bicycle camping, though not a very new idea, has recently begun to provide an alternative to all this for a great many

Americans. Like backpacking, ski touring, mountaineering, and canoeing, it has been practiced by a few strange characters all along, but suddenly a large segment of the population is beginning to discover they weren't so foolish after all. Though the equipment needed requires a significant investment, it is trifling compared to the outlay of the average car camper, to say nothing of the drivers of the huge "camping vehicles" bought by so many people in their efforts to get outdoors. Yet the bicycle is a far more versatile vehicle, particularly for recreational use. Near most urban areas these days, a camping trip isn't much fun until you've already driven for several hours. Freewheeling on a bicycle is usually a joy from the beginning.

One starts early in the morning to combine the advantages of avoiding the traffic, catching the incomparable morning air, and getting an early start on the trip. The senses are alive to the life of the world around in a way that they never are during automobile travel. The necessities of life and the means of comfort are carried in a few small packs attached to the bicycle. One is free to follow the lure of the open road at will, without significantly polluting the environment, menacing everyone about, cursing the other occupants of the road, insulating oneself from the world around, or taking up more than a fair amount of the earth's space.

What This Book Is About

This is a book about bicycle camping and secondarily about other aspects of bicycles and bicycling. It attempts to cover everything you need to know to plan a successful camping trip using a bicycle for travel, whether you are a neophyte looking for your first bike since the Schwinn you gave up at the age of twelve, an experienced cyclist who would like to start camping on weekends or vacations, or a backpacker who would like to try a different sort of self-propelled camping.

A lot of attention in this book is devoted to camping. A trip can be enjoyed whether the amount of ground covered in a day is 25 miles or 150, but it is bound to be miserable if the traveller can't keep dry on a rainy night or get himself a hot supper. Even a trained road racer will get wet at night if he can't pitch a tent. Furthermore, there is a lot of variation needed in camping techniques depending on the country and weather in which you're cycling. The actual technique of cycling, however, doesn't really change all that much from New England to the Rockies to the California coast. One simply keeps the old feet turning around and around, shifting gears to accommodate the gradient.

Some basic information is given in chapter 5 on the choice, construction, maintenance, and repair of bicycles, and for those who just want to get out onto the road, this should be adequate. For the enthusiast and the technically inclined reader, a number of excellent books have been published recently, and some recommendations on these are made in an appendix at the back of the text.

Much more space is devoted to subjects of special concern to the bicycle camper that are normally neglected in cycling literature. These range from the construction of homemade equipment for bicycle camping to the methods of planning normal and unusual trips. The beginner can easily find reams of controversy on fork rake, but hardly a line of simple advice on rainwear.

Some Limitations

The reader will find little in this volume about racing techniques or frame brazing methods. Only cursory attention is given to European-style touring, dependent on hostels, hotels and restaurants. Besides being expensive in the U.S., where hostels are generally few and far between, in many parts of the country this type of touring isn't nearly as much fun as camping. The cyclist has far less difficulty in finding campsites than the car camper. His vehicle takes up little space, can be carried over obstacles easily, and often evokes the sympathy of landowners who are approached with courtesy. Hence, the emphasis in this book is on getting out in the country and camping, rather than spending the nights at standard lodgings. These accommodations are appropriate and necessary in cities, but the bicycle camper likes to get out in the country, and revels in his independence from innkeepers.

And a Caution

The emphasis in this book will naturally be on equipment and technique. Those are what the neophyte needs a book to tell him about. They are only means, however. You don't need a thousand dollars worth of hardware to enjoy freewheeling on the open road. Since the modern bicycle is a precision piece of engineering, since racers are among the greatest enthusiasts and must naturally concern themselves greatly with equipment, and since it is to the advantage of those with a commercial interest in bicycling to emphasize hardware, there is far too much attention paid to it. There *are* important differences between a $100 bicycle and a $300 one, and the expensive bike is often worth the money, but that doesn't make it essential to the enjoyment of touring or bicycle camping. Equipment is secondary, and it should be kept in its place.

Remember that the important thing is to get out onto the road. Suck in some fresh air and get the blood pumping around in your veins while you listen to the meadowlarks and watch the sparrows flitting in the grass. You don't need much equipment to get started, especially in warm weather. Even if you have to start with an old clunker and a ten-pound sleeping bag, get out on the road this weekend, and see what you can find. Good cycling!

1

What It's All About

The growth of cycling in the U.S. in the last few years has been truly amazing, though it has not been an isolated phenomenon, since enthusiasm for many other outdoor activities has been just as great. People, or at least some of them, are tired of being bored, fat, and confined by their own world so much that they no longer experience the greater and more varied world around them. The immediate effect of this renewed enthusiasm for an old sport has been a tremendous increase in the number of bicycles on the road, accompanied by a demand for better facilities for cycling. There are even signs that some day soon people may reclaim their cities from the automobile takeover.

In the cities, the cyclist brave enough to risk the traffic can often chuckle to himself over the fact that he can travel much faster than a car through the modern urban centers. At best, however, the cities provide a hostile environment for the cyclist. He must be constantly on guard against being run down by motorists and has no choice but to breathe their exhaust. The suburbs are sometimes better, but it is out on the country roads that the freewheeling cyclist really comes into his own, gliding quietly past the fields and trees quickly enough for the changing scene to refresh, but slowly enough to see the details that give the country character and life. He can hear the voices of the frog and the cicada, and she can feel the wind on her face. They can both feel pity for the motorist who zips by unaware of the green heron standing in the marsh.

Many people have discovered some of the joys of cycling on jaunts close to home, daily commuting, or weekend trips using both an automobile and a bicycle. These approaches are satisfying, and there are outlets like racing available for those with a lust for more difficult things. For an increasing number of people, however, these styles of cycling don't really satisfy the desire for longer and more varied experience of the country aboard their bikes. They would prefer to be able to use cycles for transportation on weekend trips, vacations, or longer breaks from the routine. The tradition of bicycle touring has long been established in Europe, and interest in it is growing in North America.

European-Style Touring in the U.S.

The normal method of touring in Europe is based on a network of hostels and other inexpensive accommodations where the cyclist can spend the night, pedalling from one to another during the day. This method allows the tourist to go as far as he likes without having to carry a lot of equipment. Lightweight bedding, suitable for sleeping indoors, a few changes of clothes, and some repair items for the bike are all that he needs.

The advantages of this school of touring are obvious—the cyclist is free of the encumbrances of his possessions: hauling them, caring for them, assembling and disassembling them. He can travel with almost as little weight as if he were rolling along

The cyclist comes into his own out on the open road, where the scenery is fine and the traffic is light.

a few hours' ride from home. The American Youth Hostels in this country serve bicyclists well, and they can be used for this type of touring. There are not very many of them, however, so anyone interested in European-style touring will have to use expensive public accommodations a good bit of the time unless he has lots of strategically placed friends along his proposed route of travel.

Hopefully, there will be a lot more of this kind of touring in this country as the bicycle fraternity continues to grow. With a larger number of hostels and some commercial accommodations catering to those desiring simplicity and minimal expense, this style of travel could be a nearly ideal way to take vacations in some sections of the country. It would be perfectly suited for tours of museums, music festivals, and the like, for example, since these are located in urban areas where bicycle camping is difficult.

Still, European-style touring is never likely to displace bicycle camping in the U.S. and Canada, simply because there is so much open country out there to be explored. In the West, one can pedal all day without encountering any large towns, simply because so many of the interesting regions of the West are sparsely populated. The same trick can be managed in the East with careful planning. It is in situations like this that the bicycle camper finds his element. He can ride all day, satisfying his mood, either pedalling hard and covering over one hundred miles, or moving in a more leisurely fashion and doing lots of sightseeing. As the day comes to an end, he finds a pleasant campsite and beds down.

The bicycle camper, like the backpacker, carries his house along with him. He is not dependent on the location of accommodations, and this is the attraction of bicycle camping over touring from one hostel or hotel to another. Though he must work against an extra load and increased wind resistance, the bicycle camper can come and go as he likes. He has the freedom of the open road.

Bicycles, Backpacks, and Such

Camping by cycle has its own special niche in the world of camping and wilderness travel, standing midway between backpacking and car camping. The camping bicyclist provides his own motive power, as do the backpacker, canoeist, touring skier, and mountaineer, and so he must keep his equipment light, simple, and compact. Because he uses his own muscles to get him around and moves at moderate speeds with his body exposed to the open air (not to mention wind, rain, sleet, and snow) the bicycle camper feels far more akin to the backpacker than he does to the car camper. He can hear the rustle of the grass, watch the grasshoppers jumping in the field, and stop to marvel at the flight of a great blue heron. Engines do not separate him from the world around.

In other ways, however, cycle camping does bear more re-semblance to automobile touring than other forms of self-propelled travel. The most obvious common characteristic is the road. The bicycle camper is pretty much confined to roads. He can head across a field to camp, lift his vehicle over obstacles, and travel on some roads where cars are prohibited, but basically he uses the same highway system that automobiles do. He also has the advantages of convenient sources of supply, easy routefinding, simple planning, and readily accessible trips. The backpacker must usually travel some way to get to the start of his real trip; the bicyclist can generally start from his front porch.

A cycle camper can also travel a lot farther than a back-packer, averaging anywhere from 50 to 150 miles in a day. Thus, the cyclist generally sees a far wider variety of scenery than a backpacker out for the same length of time. He can travel past beaches, mountains, and farmland, all on the same week-end. The transition from town to countryside can be made at a satisfying speed.

Another difference between bicycle camping and backpacking is that the backpacker generally has to carry all the food for his whole trip with him, or face many complications. Supplies are hard to obtain without annoying detours, and the weight of the pack begins to cut into the pleasure of a trip that is going to last longer than two weeks. The cyclist, on the other hand, can usually buy his supplies at stores along the way, and he rarely has to carry more than a few days' provisions at any one time. This fact enables him to keep the weight of his pack fairly stable, regardless of the length of his trip.

Mixing Things Up

Bicycle camping can often be happily combined with other varieties of wilderness travel, since most lightweight camping equipment is versatile enough to be used for mountaineering, canoeing, backpacking, ski touring, bicycling, or almost any kind of self-propelled travel. This keeps expenses manageable for people who like all these types of recreation, but it also allows anyone with imagination to plan all sorts of interesting combination trips. I like to bicycle up to the trailhead before a climb in the Rockies, for example. Bicycles can be used for a lot of nice circuit trips in conjunction with canoes or backpacks. One can stash the bicycles at the end of a river run, and then use them to get back to the car, rather than relying on hitchhiking or on some poor soul who is stuck with the driving while others canoe. Long backpacking trips which start at one roadhead and end at another become easier to arrange and more fun to boot, when the trip in the opposite direction is made by bicycle.

Bicycle camping is also readily combined with all sorts of other objectives from art tours of Europe to wine excursions to California vineyards. Possibilities are limited only by your imagination.

Getting Started

Though bicycle camping can be as challenging as one wants to make it, it is not hard for the beginner to start, providing he takes things a step at a time. Some equipment is essential, but one can make do in many areas, providing goals are set accordingly. With good weather and level ground, the beginner can have a lot of fun with scrounged-up equipment, until he can afford to get the things he needs to handle longer trips in rougher weather and terrain. This approach will also get the neophyte in better shape for bigger trips and will give him more knowledge of his real needs when he comes around to buying his outfit.

Even though it is possible to enjoy trips of fifteen miles on an old one-speed, ten-ton Columbia, combined with a monster car-camping sleeping bag, ultimately anyone very interested in bicycle camping will want an outfit more suited to the sport. This equipment is expensive, and it is getting costlier every day. One of the main purposes of this book is to help those who want to start bicycle camping to spend their money wisely. There are some good places to cut corners, and there are also ways to engage in very false economy.

The first item of equipment for the bicycle camper is, of course, a bicycle. This is also the item on which he should skimp the least. Though he can get by with a one- or three-speed clunker, anyone really interested in bicycle camping will be a lot happier in the long run with a decent ten- or fifteen-speed touring machine.

People who already have other kinds of bicycles in reasonable mechanical condition may want to start touring with them, picking up some camping equipment first, and then working up to better bicycles later. Those who are going to go out and buy bicycles, however, should spend the money and the effort required to get good ones.

Bicycles are discussed in some detail in chapter 5, with special attention to choosing a touring bike, so there is no point in repeating the information here. It is worth pointing out, however, that the more time the novice (or expert) spends reading about

A basic set-up for bicycle camping. This equipment is adequate for weeks of camping in the mountains.

bikes, shopping around, and comparing features by looking and test riding, the more likely he is to be happy with his choice for years to come.

If a touring bike is also going to be ridden around town, to work, or anywhere else that it might be left unattended for even a short time, *a good lock and chain should be purchased.* Thefts of bicycles are skyrocketing everywhere, and there is no improvement in sight.

The next item of equipment should be at least one good carrier. Though it is possible to use a backpack for bicycle camping, it is a poor idea for a number of reasons. Panniers and many other items can be improvised at first, but one has to have some way to attach equipment to the bicycle, and that means a carrier.

Other items of camping equipment can be improvised at first, depending on the conditions expected on the tour. Those who are just getting started shouldn't overlook the possibility of renting some equipment, in order to spread major purchases over a longer period. Money can be spent first on those things which can't be begged, borrowed, bypassed, or rented.

First Trips

For most people the key to enjoying cycle camping is to take it easy at first. The meaning of the phrase will vary a great deal depending on experience, conditioning, and temperament, but the first few trips at least should be well within the capacity of the weakest member of the party. Those who have done lots of cycling for longer distances on one-day trips may want to make ambitious excursions from the start, but others should plan on very short, leisurely rambles on their first couple of weekends.

Unless they are experienced lightweight campers, newcomers to bicycle camping should plan to get into camp by mid-afternoon, with at least three hours to go before dark. Until practice has made setting up camp quick and easy, getting in late is no fun at all, especially after a hard day of pedalling. Learning the ropes is a lot more fun by daylight, with plenty of time left over for cooking supper and washing up before nightfall.

Those who have not spent much time cycling will also find that a few day trips for training will form a worthwhile foundation for the first weekend camping trip. There is a lot of technique involved in just pedalling long distances, and besides this there are often mechanical problems that need to be worked out on the bicycle. The physical capacities of all the members of a party need to be understood by anyone planning a tour lasting a weekend or longer.

Beginning or experienced cyclists should remember that riding with a load is much harder than cruising along without one, especially if hills or headwinds are encountered. There is a big difference between riding a hundred miles with no more baggage than a water bottle, a lunch, and a windbreaker, and doing the same distance with camping equipment for a week-long trip. Another common mistake is to assume that if one can ride a certain distance on a Sunday trip, he can expect to do the same every day on a long journey. Besides needing time for camp chores, especially if they are inexperienced, most people can't enjoy maintaining their maximum pace day after day, at least not during the first week.

The best way to get started at bicycle camping is to get out on the road, but ambitions should be kept on short rein for the first few tours. A lot of time should be spent planning ahead of time—checking the route and campsites, getting equipment together, and making sure that everything is in order. Later on, all these things become second nature, but for the neophyte, careful attention to them will save lots of discomfort on his first few trips.

2

Camping Along The Road

The special satisfaction of bicycle *camping,* as opposed to other methods of touring, lies in the fact that the camper carries everything he needs on his bike. He isn't dependent on reservations or hospitality. He sets his own schedule. The pleasant sense of relative self-sufficiency and the feeling of the freedom of the road can be much greater for the camping cyclist.

Many beginning cycle campers come to grief because they fail to think of cycle camping as an art in itself. Usually they are cyclists who do a lot of town riding or one-day trips and want to get out on longer journeys, for weekends or vacations. This is a good reason for two-wheel camping, but it often leads to a sloppy attitude and a lot of miserable nights.

The touring cyclist covers a lot of ground during the day. Poorly chosen equipment can make them far more arduous, increasing wind resistance and weight, unbalancing the bike, spoiling the critical rhythm of the rider and causing mechanical troubles.

Even more trying for such ill-prepared campers, though, are the uncomfortable nights which frequently result from their lack of foresight. There is nothing so pleasant as a good meal on the fire and a warm, soft bed waiting after a hard day's ride—and nothing quite so miserable as a poor meal and a cold, wet sleeping bag under the same circumstances.

The main purpose of a bicycle camping trip is usually the bicycling, but the camping is what makes the experience a delight or an ordeal. A well-cooked meal and a restful night's sleep will gloss over a lot of miseries during the day, from rain to surly drivers. But memories of unappetizing meals and sleepless nights are likely to sour the best riding days.

Camping Basics

The essence of bicycle camping is simply to live in reasonable comfort along the road with what one can carry readily on his bike. The main requirements are that one have adequate shelter from the elements, a bed warm enough and comfortable enough to allow him to sleep well, clothing that will keep him warm and dry in camp, food and cooking equipment that will enable him to prepare satisfying meals, and necessities for personal hygiene.

All this may seem like a great deal, but with modern materials and equipment design, coupled with efficient camping technique, it can be very light indeed. On a recent week-long tour in the Rockies, where the possibility of inclement weather at high altitude requires a heavier-than-average load, my whole bicycle weighed only 45 pounds, including all my equipment, extra clothes, and supplies other than food purchased on the road.

Lightweight camping requires careful planning, if it is also going to be comfortable. Equipment needs are heavily dependent on the area and circumstances in which one is travelling. If wood and suitable spots are available one can depend on fires for cooking, but otherwise it will be necessary to carry a stove and fuel. The climate will determine the weight of the sleeping bag which needs to be carried. The sort of campsite available may dictate what type ground bed is required under the sleeping bag. Where frequent heavy rains are the rule, a tent is usually necessary, but if only occasional precipitation is anticipated, an emergency shelter may be more than adequate. The first camping skill to be learned is planning.

While planning for a bicycle tour, the most important fact to keep in mind is that light weight is the key to an enjoyable trip. Nonessential weight has to be pared off ruthlessly. Every extra ounce has to be pushed along for mile after mile. Every extra package tied onto the bicycle means added wind resistance to be worked against.

Choosing a Campsite

The spot where camp is to be made may be chosen long in advance on a map checked at home, it may be picked from the vantage point of the bicycle seat as the muscles start to flag in the late afternoon, or the choice may be made somewhere in between. If some kind of a rigid schedule is going to be followed on the tour, if large numbers of people are involved, or if campsites are few or crowded, it is usually advisable to make the choice well in advance, perhaps making reservations as well. When possible, however, the vagabond approach is often more pleasant—there is a particular satisfaction in coming across a fine lake in the afternoon and stopping there for the night just because it is such a perfect spot.

The first step in planning a camping routine requires finding out what sort of rules and situations govern camping in the area where one is travelling. In National Forests, National Parks, and other federally and state-owned land, this usually is a simple matter of writing to the appropriate government agency. Many reference books and maps are also available which show the regularly established campgrounds and give general information about them. The less developed ones and those which are relatively remote are usually more suitable for the cyclist. It is also often perfectly alright to camp on publicly owned land, providing certain regulations are abided by. In the case of privately owned land, it is both courteous and prudent to check with the owner before you begin pitching your tent. Farmers and other landowners have quite a different attitude towards guests who consult with them first, and buckshot makes poor waterproofing for a tent. When you do ask permission to camp on someone's land, be sure you come to an understanding on whether you are allowed to build a fire and on other points of etiquette, such as late night noise. Avoid misunderstandings, and leave everything cleaner than you found it, so that you will be welcome back.

There is also a great limbo of unattended land, some privately owned, such as areas being held for speculation, and some public property, like the rights-of-way along superhighways. Though such places are rarely ideal campsites, you may sometimes end up staying in them, when you are caught short of your goal by a thunderstorm, for example. It is best to be as unobtrusive as possible in such spots, avoiding fires, pitching camp well away from roads and dwellings, and asking permission of anyone who might live nearby. A neighbor who might be alarmed by someone moving into the adjoining wood may be positively protective of those who are considerate of him. It is also wise to check the trespass laws of the area in which you are travelling and to ask the local police if you are in doubt. If you get advance permission, you are less likely to be rousted in the middle of the night.

The Ideal Campsite

Since a great many of the most important features of a camping spot are aesthetic, everyone's ideal site will be different, but there are many common features possessed by any spot likely to be considered highly by an experienced bicycle camper. Drinking water should be readily available. In the case of organized campgrounds, the references should say whether or not water is available. Running water that can be reached by the cyclist should be assumed to be polluted unless proven otherwise. Looks are deceiving and should not be relied upon.

A good campsite should have adequate drainage and be located away from mosquito bogs. It should have water available and a fireplace if needed, and, ideally, it should be a pleasant place.

If a fire is to be built, the campsite should have a fireplace or a spot where mineral soil can be reached. Fires must never be built on peat, forest duff, or other flammable bases. The remains of a fire can smolder for weeks deep in such material, bursting into flame again much later. The fireplace must also be a safe distance from any flammable material, with the meaning of "safe" dependent on wind conditions and fire hazard. When the danger of fire is very high, stoves should be used for cooking, whether fires are legally banned or not.

A level spot which is not too rocky should be available for sleeping, with other desirable characteristics dependent on one's shelter. With a tube tent, one looks for a spot in a direct line between two objects suitable for anchoring the line, while with a conventional tent one searches for ground in which the stakes will be easy to drive. For sleeping out under the stars, one may spend time looking for an attractive frame of trees to look up at while falling asleep.

In any case, it is wise to avoid mosquito hollows, runoff channels where the rain falling on the whole campground will drain, hard gravel pads designed for three-ton camping machines, and the path to the outhouse. If insects present a problem, try to find a high, airy spot, where the evening breezes will eliminate at least some of the pests.

Obviously, in warmer seasons at least, it is nice to have a lake or river where swimming is allowed, where the day's road grit can be washed off and tired muscles can relax before supper. If all these criteria can be met and a view is included without a large crowd, the campsite is just about as nearly perfect as anything on this earth.

Organized Campgrounds

Campgrounds are operated by the U.S. Forest Service, the U.S. Park Service, occasionally by other Federal agencies, by state park and forestry departments, by municipalities and large land-owning concerns like lumber companies, and by private individuals and groups operating such facilities for a profit. Information concerning the governmentally operated facilities can be obtained from the appropriate agencies, and books listing most campgrounds can be gotten from many sources, including oil companies and auto clubs. Unfortunately, most such guides are designed with the owners of huge "campers", trailers, and similar vehicles in mind, but the bicyclist can extrapolate the information he needs. He should be sure to check to see whether reservations are needed.

Fees for camping at organized facilities vary a great deal. Those at privately run grounds are usually fairly high, partly because the owners naturally want to make a profit, and partly because the cyclist is liable to end up paying for some of the services provided to the overmechanized campers around him. Campgrounds run under other auspices may be free, may charge nominal camping fees, or may be as high-priced as privately operated ones. Cyclists who are touring on a tight budget should check in advance if they wish to avoid expensive surprises.

If you plan to stay often on Federal land, be sure to check in advance to see if the Golden Eagle program is currently in effect. This program allows one to pay a reasonable annual fee for the use or price reductions at all federally operated facilities.

One should expect to find rather hard ground at the campsites in most organized campgrounds. They tend more and more to be designed with the users of large recreational vehicles in mind, and the sites, particularly in large campgrounds, often consist of gravel pads. These are usually strong enough to hold a Mack truck and are impeccably level, so that the water in milady's sink will not tilt, but they are horrible tent sites. When planning to camp in such places, it is advisable to carry some spikes for tent stakes, since it is often impossible to drive anything else.

Shelters

Tents and other shelters seem basic to camping, even though one can sometimes dispense with them. The tent or its surrogate is the camper's home away from home. With a good tent, the cyclist can be cozy despite driving rain, sleet, or snow, and some of his happiest moments are likely to be spent sitting under a fabric shelter in front of the cooking fire or nursing a little gasoline stove in the comfort of his portable home.

In choosing a tent design, either for a ready-made tent or one he's making himself, the bicyclist must consider his needs very carefully. An ideal tent for one use can be very poor for many others. No tent is perfect in all circumstances, but a camper who has a tent which is good for most of his purposes and adequate for all of them is doing very well. Tent design is considered in more detail in the next chapter.

Sometimes, cycle tours can be planned using existing shelters, such as the lean-tos provided at some organized campgrounds. Where the weather is sufficiently stable and dry, or where there are enough natural shelters, it may also be possible to leave one's portable shelters at home. As a rule, however, the bicycle camper will have to carry at least a rudimentary covering with him, since if he doesn't, the storm is bound to catch him far from the nearest hostel or overhanging rock.

Shelters Other Than Tents

In addition to tents, the choice of which is discussed in the following chapter, there are a number of simpler portable shelters which are often admirably suited to the needs of the bicycle camper. Tarpaulins of various sizes and materials can be pitched in numerous ways, some of which are illustrated. A poncho can also be used for shelter, in addition to being a rain garment. It is essentially a small tarp with a head-hole and hood. Tube tents, which consist simply of long tubes of plastic or waterproof fabric, are justly popular, since one can be rigged simply by stringing a line between two objects.

Probably the simplest and least expensive shelter for the beginning bicycle camper is a plastic tube tent. One- and two-occupant sizes can be purchased in either clear or opaque plastic for $2 - $5. This type of shelter is ideal for areas where long periods of rain or cold are not common, and it is excellent for the beginner because of its low cost and the ease with which one can learn to use it. A one-man tube tent is usually made of a nine-foot length of four-mil thick plastic sheeting, which comes in the form of a tube ten feet in diameter. Typically, one would pitch it by simply running a length of nylon parachute cord through the tube and tying the ends from two trees. The tube is then held open by the cord. The camper beds down inside the tube, and his weight prevents it from being blown around. The ends are left open for ventilation. A tube should be pitched across the prevailing wind.

In the long list of camping equipment the beginner will want to purchase, a tent will normally come near the end, and a tube

A two-man tube tent made of transparent plastic. This one is tied into the seat of the bicycle, providing both support for the tent and security for the bike. The clothespins are useful in wind or blowing rain. This tube withstood winds of 50 miles per hour.

Staking the wheels of the bike with U-shaped alloy stakes can stabilize it when it is used to support a shelter, as in the previous picture and the tarp method shown in the next chapter. It is also useful to hold up the bike, as illustrated in Chapter VI.

tent can be used to fill the gap for some time, even in climates where it is less than ideal. Its disadvantages are that it tends to condense moisture inside, which then runs down the walls and pools in the bottom, and that the open ends are vulnerable to wind driven rain and surface run-off. It is also most unsuited to use in cold weather, requires outside anchors at least three or four feet high, and has a relatively short useful life. Fabric tube tents have all the same virtues and vices, except that they have a somewhat higher initial cost and a much longer life.

Tarps have similar advantages and disadvantages. They are very light, and their cost is low. They are somewhat more versatile than tube tents, but require a bit more skill and imagination to use effectively. Many experienced lightweight campers never use any other shelter. There are various dimensions which work well, but 9′ by 11′ is probably as good as any. Numerous grommets and ties are helpful in pitching a tarp in different ways. In using a plastic tarp, special clamps can be used, or a small object like a stone can be tied off at the desired place, methods which can also be used with cloth where a grommet or tie is missing.

Using a stone to provide a tie point on a tarpaulin. The method can be used with plastic tarps as well.

Cooking on the Road

One of the most important skills for a beginning bicycle camper to master if he is to feel really happy about travelling around on two wheels is that of cooking enjoyable meals. For most people, uninteresting food takes all the joy out of a trip after the first few days on the road. Interest in even the most spectacular scenery is likely to pall at the thought of yet another plate of hot dogs and canned beans. Yet there really isn't any need for dull food while bicycle camping. The cook has everything working for him. Finicky appetites are rare after a hard day's ride. Food can be purchased along the way, so the bicyclist doesn't have nearly so much of a problem with weight and spoilage as the backpacker. Finally, modern equipment and food processing make cooking in camp much easier and allow far more variety in the choice of a menu than the old-timers ever had.

The need for planning menus in advance varies a lot with one's skill as a cook, the sort of area in which one is touring, and the size of the group. A talented camp cook can concoct a meal on the spur of the moment, without a lot of advance thought about ingredients and quantities. The beginner, however, will be far more successful if he carries along lists of planned meals, ingredients, recipes, and cooking items. Otherwise, he is all too likely to realize that the most essential item was forgotten, twenty-five miles after the stop at the market. Similarly, on trips through country where stores are small, expensive, and far apart, most supplies will be carried, and more planning will be required. Careful advance preparation is always necessary for large groups of cyclists.

The first item which needs consideration in planning a menu is the cooking equipment and methods. When the cooking is done over a campfire, several dishes can easily be kept going at the same time. On the other hand, if cooking is done on a stove, only one pan at a time can be heated, and the menu should be adjusted accordingly. Some special dishes may also require special utensils—blueberry muffins can only be baked if a reflector oven or similar device is carried, for example.

A good deal of consideration should be given to the trip when the menu is planned. On summer tours through farm country, only a cook completely devoid of gastronomic feeling could pass all those fresh fruit and vegetable stands to prepare a meal using exclusively dehydrated foods. When sources for fresh food will be passed only a few times on a long trip, the cook should make full use of perishables when they are available, in order to stave off the craving for fresh foods that is bound to follow a few weeks of a diet consisting exclusively of preserved foods. Dehydrated foods must make up the bulk of the menu on trips where few stores will be passed. Fresh foods and canned goods are too heavy and bulky to be carried in quantity on the bicycle. Consideration should also be given to ease of preparation in connection with the style of travel intended. A party making a leisurely sojourn and stopping at camp early in the afternoon can afford to plan meals taking a couple of hours to cook, if they like. However, when the day's travel pushes through late afternoon, growling stomachs and frayed nerves will greet any delays in the speedy preparation of supper once camp has finally been reached.

In general, on a bicycle camping trip supplies can be purchased every day or two, so that the weight of food carried can be kept down. Usually, condiments and some supplies that may be hard to obtain at local markets are carried regardless of the frequency of supermarkets along the route. Some staples may also be carried in limited quantities, so that they can be purchased in economical sizes. Aside from these items, however, a group of bicycle campers usually stops at the last convenient source of groceries that is passed before reaching camp. When there is a supermarket within a couple of hours' ride from camp, groceries can be bought without much regard for weight and spoilage. In more remote areas, with two or three days' ride to the next supply point, considerable prudence has to be exercised in order to keep weight and bulk at a minimum.

One-pot Meals

The one-pot meal is a basic method of camp cookery, particularly when small, single-burner stoves are being used. It is a

Using a cooker to prepare a one-pot meal. The pannier is being used as a wind shield.

technique that is particularly useful for beginners and for those who feel they have limited talents for cooking, but it is also the method of choice used by many superb roadside chefs. Variations can easily be allowed depending on the availability of fresh corn-on-the-cob or steak, but many of the best menus for bicycle camping are based primarily on the one-pot meal.

Soups, stews, goulashes, casseroles, and such are all in this category, and many favorite dishes of this type that are used at home can be easily modified for camp use. In camp such food is nearly always boiled, so more water will probably be necessary than for the same dish when it is baked in an oven. The extra fluid is generally welcome in the cyclist's diet anyway, since the day's pedalling normally leaves everyone somewhat dehydrated.

A basic one-pot meal usually has a base of rice, potatoes, noodles, spaghetti, macaroni, bulgar wheat, beans, or something similar. Some combinations of staples will provide adequate complete protein, but more often a protein source like meat, fish, or cheese is added, along with appropriate vegetables and condiments. The order of cooking will, of course, depend on the ingredients. Here are a few recipes to get you started. Quantities should be multiplied by the number of people being fed. Portions are generous.

Veal Casserole

½ lb. frozen or fresh veal
Small quantity flour in plastic bag (optional)
2 T margarine or other fat
3-4 stalks celery
1 small onion (or 1 T dehydrated onion)
1 small can mushrooms or equivalent dried mushrooms
1 small (4 oz.) can evaporated milk
½ cup rice
1 cup water
Soy sauce to taste
Other spices as desired (for example, sage, garlic, marjoram, basil)
Salt and pepper to taste

Cut veal into small chunks and shake in flour if desired. Heat fat in bottom of pan and sauté meat, celery, onion, and mushrooms until meat is browned. Add milk, water, rice, 1T soy sauce, ½ t salt, a dash of pepper, and any additional seasoning desired. Stir. Bring to boil, cover, and cook at low boil for 30 minutes. Season to taste.

Meatballs and Potatoes au Randonneur

½ lb. ground beef or 1 can meatballs
1 small onion, chopped
½ t sage
½ t garlic salt
⅛ t pepper
½ t marjoram
½ t oregano
1 T margerine or other fat
½ pkg. gravy mix
2 cups water
1 pkg. frozen peas (optional)
1 small can (4 oz.) evaporated milk

¼ lb. cheddar or parmesan cheese
1 cup dried mashed potato flakes
2 T margerine or butter

Mix spices and onion into meat, form into balls, and fry in hot fat in bottom of pan until thoroughly cooked. Stir gravy mix into fat and then add water slowly over heat, stirring so that no lumps are formed. Bring to a boil, add peas if used, and simmer 5 minutes. Add milk and cheese and bring to boil again. Remove from heat, stir in potatoes and margarine, re-cover, and allow to stand 5 minutes.

Tuna Velosport

1¼ cup water
½ t salt
½ cup bulgar wheat (Ala, parboiled wheat)
1 T margarine
1 can of tuna fish (6-7 oz.)
¼ lb. cheddar cheese, diced or grated
⅛ t pepper
1 T paprika
1 - 8 oz. container sour cream or imitation sour cream
Handful of raw or roasted cashews (optional)

Bring water to a boil, add salt and margarine, and stir in bulgar wheat. Bring to a boil again, cover, and simmer for 15 minutes. Stir in tuna, cheese, and spices, and reheat. Stir in sour cream and cashews.

Soups, Salads and Such

Besides one-pot meals, all sorts of other items can be used for camp cooking, but some dishes are especially useful. When fresh vegetables are available, salads are particularly refreshing, and they work into the routine of camping very well, since a salad can be made while other things are cooking, even if only one stove is available. In hot weather, salads often make a pleasant main course, with tuna, canned meat, cheese, cottage cheese, nuts, beans, or yogurt providing a source of protein.

Soup is often very welcome when one first arrives at camp, serving to stave off hunger while the initial camp chores are attended to, and also providing some salty fluids to make up for some of the perspiration expended during the day. Dried soup packets serve this purpose well and also make good flavorings for one-pot meals.

When stores are encountered frequently, canned, fresh, or frozen fruit makes very welcome desserts requiring no preparation, while instant puddings will satisfy this purpose in the farther reaches.

Hot drinks are usually managed most easily by keeping a pot of hot water on and carrying the materials for a variety of instant drinks—tea, coffee, boullion, and hot chocolate. Many cold drinks, including fruit juices, are available in powdered form.

Fires and Stoves

The first step in cooking a meal is, of course, to produce the necessary heat. A fire is always pleasant at camp, besides serving culinary purposes, but whether one chooses to rely on fires will depend on a number of factors. They may or may not be permitted, depending on the location of the tour, the time of year, and the condition of the woods. A fire permit may be required, even for stoves, and inquiry should always be made to the appropriate authorities to check on current regulations and to obtain the necessary permission. Remember that fire regulations are made for good reasons and that heavy fines are often imposed on violators.

Regardless of regulations, it is important to realize that most bicycle camping is done in regions of heavy use, simply because bicyclists camp near the roads. Only dead wood should be collected, and existing fireplaces should be used when possible to avoid making new fire scars. Fires must be built only on mineral bases, with all flammable debris removed from around the fireplace. Never build fires on peat or forest duff, since smoldering embers can lie buried deep in such material for long periods before bursting into flame long after you have gone. There is also no excuse for killing live plants merely to make a fire. A stove should be carried if there is any doubt about the availability of firewood or about whether fires will be permitted.

If the cyclist is caught without a stove and fires are prohibited or dead wood is not available, he must make the best of a cold meal or head for the nearest hot dog stand.

Cyclists camping on private land or away from established sites should be particularly wary of making cooking fires. No matter how careful the camper may be with fires, he must remember that local property owners and authorities have no way of knowing his conservative attitude—too many fires in the past have been started by careless campers. Unless one knows that people around will not mind, it is best to use a stove when camping away from regular campgrounds.

For all the reasons just mentioned, carry a small stove whenever there is any doubt about the feasibility of fires on a trip. Very efficient small stoves burning white gasoline and weighing just over a pound are available from stores specializing in backpacking and mountaineering equipment. Stoves using pressurized gas weigh only slightly more. Population pressure has simply made the use of fires obsolete in many areas where gathering wood can only disfigure the environment campers go to enjoy, and cyclists should expect to rely increasingly on stoves for cooking in heavily used spots.

Cooking Over a Fire

As long as reasonably dry fuel is available, the technique of building a fire is quite simple. One method is shown in the accompanying series of illustrations. The usual mistake made by beginners is to try to rush things by omitting a few steps in the progression from small material to large or by not gathering enough fuel before starting. To start, the fire must have plenty of fuel and plenty of air—single sticks will not burn well alone, but neither will a bunch which is packed too tightly.

One may choose to carry some commercially available fire starter, but he should practice starting fires without their aid. Practice is what enables experienced people to start fires in wet conditions. Gasoline should never be used as a fire starter; it's dangerous. One of the simplest and most effective starters is a

The main trick in building a fire is to gather enough fuel of each size before trying to light anything. In the first picture dry wood of various sizes is gathered next to the fireplace. Some of it is used to build an initial stack, with tiny twigs on the bottom and larger ones on top. There must be plenty of air space and plenty of extra wood. With practice the fire can be started with one match—this one was.

cigarette lighter, but some matches should be carried in a waterproof container in case the lighter goes the way of all gadgets just when it is needed.

Once a fire is going well, wet wood can be dried out beside it and burned after the drying. The trick is to get enough dry wood to start the fire at the beginning. Small dead twigs on trees, especially near the trunk, are often dry enough for kindling, but one may have to do a lot of searching to find larger pieces that are reasonably dry. If a fire is planned, it is wise to gather some wood well before reaching camp if it starts to rain. This can be wrapped in something to keep it dry, so that getting a fire started is not such a chore. Morning firewood should be stored in a dry place the night before. After long periods of really wet weather, dry wood may be impossible to get without an axe, the latter being used to split the dry centers out of logs or stubs. It is rarely worthwhile to carry an axe on bicycle trips, however, so in these conditions the stove is usually relied on.

If there is no fireplace already built, one should be constructed with stones. The fireplace will help to control drafts, reflect heat, and support cooking pots. If much cooking is done over fires, it is simplest to carry a light grate along to hold pans. Otherwise the fireplace can be built with a narrow space so that pans can be put over the fire with some stability. It is a rather frustrating but common experience to have a pan precariously balanced over a couple of stones or logs go pitching into the fire just as the stew is ready. Some small but effective grates are available that weigh only about three ounces.

The fire now going, the cook usually puts on a couple of pans of water and continues with other chores while they are heating. If two pots of water are put on, one can be used for drinks and refilled as necessary, while the other is for the one-pot meal. If the latter is to be a stew made with fresh meat, the meat may be browned first in hot fat at the bottom of the pan, before water is put in.

The cooking fire should be kept reasonably small; there is no need for a large flame, which only makes tending the food more trouble while consuming more wood. The fire can be built up after supper for general good cheer. The best cooking fires consist of hardwood coals, but this fact is largely of academic interest since hardwood is rarely available around campgrounds, anyway.

While the fire is going, constant attention must be paid to wind and sparks, particularly if surrounding wood or grassland is dry. For the lone camper this means doing all the chores which would take him out of sight of the fire in advance of actually building it. It is nearly always illegal to leave a fire unattended, and for good reason. Obviously, before it is left, a fire must be drowned out, stirred, drowned and stirred again, and checked as cold to the touch.

Cooking Over a Stove

Cooking over a stove is in some ways more convenient than using a fire. Wood does not have to be gathered, fireplaces need not be built, soot does not build up on pans, and the stove is merely turned off instead of needing to be doused. Fire hazards and environmental damage are almost nil. On the other hand, cooking over a single burner presents certain problems, since two pans cannot be heated at the same time. The sequence and planning of cooking are therefore more important.

The stove should be well-protected from the wind, otherwise even if the flame does not blow out, most of the heat will be carried off directly into the great wide world rather than passing through the food on the way. Besides being sheltered, the spot should have a stable base and be out of the general line of travel, lest the pot of stew end up spilled on the ground.

The method of lighting the stove will depend on its type. With a stove using pressurized gas cylinders, the valve is simply opened while a lighted match is held to the burner. Stoves using either white gasoline or kerosene require more elaborate treatment. The fuel must come out of the orifice in gaseous form, and this is accomplished by having the liquid fuel run first through a heated tube. Before the stove will run properly, the tube must be heated and the tank must be pressurized so that the liquid fuel will be driven through the tube.

Some of the larger stoves using liquid fuel have pumps on the tanks. With one of this type the tank is first pressurized with perhaps twenty rapid strokes of the pump. If the stove is fueled with gasoline the valve can then be opened until the cup is filled with liquid fuel. The valve is closed, and the gasoline is lighted and allowed to burn down. The valve is then opened again and the burner reignited if necessary. The stove will then usually settle down after a minute or two to the steady roar of a blue cooking flame. A kerosene stove is started in the same manner except that the preliminary heating must be accomplished with some separately carried alcohol rather than with fuel from the main tank.

The lighter stoves using white gasoline are self-pressurizing. That is, the pressure which helps to drive the fuel up to the burner is produced by the heat of the stove itself, rather than by a pump. The starting procedure is the same as for a pumped stove, except that of course there is no initial pressure in the

A typical small, self-pressurizing stove using white gas or naphtha.

tank to drive the priming fuel into the cup. Several methods can be used to start the process: the tank can be heated with the warmth of the hands, with a wooden match held underneath, or with some other external flame used carefully to heat the stove a little, thus allowing the rest of the procedure outlined above to be followed; an eyedropper can be carried and used to take a bit of gas from the tank or fuel bottle, and this gas can then be put in the fuel cup for priming; gasoline can also be sloshed into any of the little recesses on the stove provided for this purpose and lighted to pressurize the tank, after which the stove can be started in the manner already described.

The purchaser of one of the small gasoline stoves should follow the printed instructions of the manufacturer which accompany a new stove and try lighting it a few times at home (outdoors) before trusting it on a trip, since there is a knack to getting one going, and hungry companions on a rainy afternoon may be somewhat impatient of the learning process. It is best to avoid those methods of lighting stoves which rely on large amounts of gasoline being used to preheat the stove, because such methods ultimately cook the wick which feeds the gasoline up to the burner, making it work less efficiently, and also because of the fire hazard involved if the stove has to be started sometime inside a tent.

If a full pot of water is first boiled on the stove, everyone can have a hot drink and then the remainder, with additions if necessary, can be used to start the main part of the meal.

Other Cooking Tips

In addition to extra liquid, cyclists are generally short on salt after a day's ride, especially in hot weather. Quite a bit of this salt can be replenished in the evening meal. Considerable quantities of margarine or butter can be added to one-pot meals to improve the flavor and provide needed calories. After the main part of the meal has been cooked, another pot of water should be put on for hot drinks. Any that is left over will be needed for washing dishes anyway.

In planning for trips made at higher altitude, it is important to remember that the boiling point of water goes down as one gets farther above sea level. The effect that this has on cooking time varies with the food, but at 5,000 feet, food will cook significantly more slowly, and at 10,000 feet some foods will take twice as long to cook as they do at sea level, while others will take three or four times as long. Above 10,000 feet, some foods will not cook by boiling at all.

Breakfasts are very much a matter of personal taste, and people are generally much less willing to modify their prejudices in the morning than they are at other times of day. Whoever plans the food for a trip should make sure that he checks everyone's preferences. Cold breakfasts are obviously the simplest to make and clean up, so if pancakes or eggs are wanted, extra time will have to be allowed. Special egg containers are available to prevent breakage. On trips farther afield, when dehydrated eggs must be used, flavorings like cheese and onions go a long way to improve the taste. An omelet is a good variation on one-pot meals for the evening.

Lunches

Some general agreement is needed within a group on the subject of lunch, so that everyone is happy with the stopping place, but this meal is left largely to the individual. In relatively civilized areas, lunch is usually purchased at a conveniently located stand or market, whether it consists of a hot dog, fresh tomatoes, or a can of smoked oysters. When several days are spent away from towns, items must be carried which keep well and are not too heavy. Nuts, sausages, cheese, tinned meat and fish, peanut butter, dried fruit, candy, and jerky are favorites. Some people like to cook some soup or make a hot drink at lunchtime, especially when the weather is chilly.

Water

Unfortunately, very few of the streams and lakes that the touring cyclist encounters are fit to drink without treatment, and even when they are, there is usually no easy way to be sure, except by risking illness. Many beautiful clear-running brooks are polluted quite well enough to put the careless bicyclist flat on his back for the rest of his vacation. Unless one is quite sure that the water of a creek or pond is safe, either because there is no human habitation or area of heavy use in the watershed above or because it has been tested by authorities and pronounced safe, it is foolish to take chances. Normally, the water supply needed during the day is carried in bottles on the bike, and these are refilled at gas stations, stores, or houses along the way. One way of obtaining the evening supply when there is no source of uncontaminated water at the campground is to carry collapsible containers or lightweight plastic jugs and to fill them before reaching camp.

Lists of designated campgrounds usually state whether water is available, but in the winter, spring, and fall, cyclists should remember that such sources are usually shut off during the period that freezing weather is possible. At campgrounds high in the mountains, the water supply will be shut off earlier in the year and turned on later.

When possibly contaminated water has to be used, it can be made safe in one of three ways: by boiling, chemical purification, or filtration. Water that is very cloudy or heavy with sediment should first be made relatively clear by allowing the sediment to settle or by filtering through cloth, cotton, or nylon floss. The water can then be purified by boiling it for twenty minutes. Boiling is certainly simplest for cooking water, since the food can be cooked at the same time. If boiling is not convenient, purification tablets may be used, a method which is especially helpful during the day when one is travelling. One Halazone or Globaline tablet whould be dissolved in each quart of water, which should then be left a half-hour before use. If the water is cloudy or still contains sediment, this dose should be doubled. After the water has stood for 30 minutes, the container should be uncapped and checked for the odor of iodine (with Globaline) or chlorine (with Halazone). If no odor is present, the treatment should be repeated.

The third method of purification is relatively new and will

not be necessary for most bicyclists, but it would be worth consideration to anyone planning a trip to areas of Mexico, Central
and South America, or other parts of the world where water
supplies in general must be considered unsafe, especially where
amoebic cysts may be present. (These are resistant to chemical
treatment.) A Millipore filtering arrangement is used, and must
be purchased specially. It consists of a bag for the water supply,
which passes through a series of tubes and filters, the last of
which has very tiny pores that will filter out bacteria and cysts
(but not viruses). A small system will cost around twenty or
twenty-five dollars.

Carrying supplementary water (in addition to the one or two
bottles for personal use during the day) presents some problems,
because most containers do not attach readily to a bicycle. If
you have enough room in your panniers, this is of no concern,
but otherwise either a large *bota* or the long flat plastic water bag,
having handles on both ends and holding 2½ gallons seems best
adapted to bicycle use, because either fits easily on a carrier. The
other alternative, for carrying water a few miles to camp, is to use
a large collapsible container carried in a backpack.

Cooking and Eating Utensils

Tools for cooking and eating should be kept simple. For personal items, a cup, a bowl, a knife, fork and spoon set, and
perhaps a plate should be plenty, and many cyclists prefer to
carry only a cup and spoon. Three pots, the largest holding
about six quarts, should be more than adequate for four people,
and one of these can be eliminated easily for a party of one or
two. Those travelling alone will find that two pans are adequate
for cooking, and will serve for plate and bowl as well. Cups
should be plastic, stainless steel, or enameled. Tinned and aluminum cups conduct heat too readily and tend to burn the lips.
One or two cooking spoons can be carried with the pots, at least
one of which should have a cover. If any significant amount of
frying is going to be done, a reasonably light steel frying pan

should be carried, since aluminum pans will burn food too easily. A spatula may also be wanted.

A combination salt and pepper shaker that can be closed to
prevent spills can be carried in the cook kit, along with a couple
of pot grippers like those shown in the illustration. Pot cleaners
also fit here, together with an all-purpose liquid bio-degradable
soap. All those drink mixes and condiments may also fit into the
cook set, where they can be easily found. If no can-opener is
included on a pocketknife, a tiny G.I. can-opener is efficient
and weighs almost nothing.

Choosing a Stove

Most bicycle campers these days will find that they need a
stove at least some of the time. Except for use by large groups, a
small backpacker's stove is generally best suited to the
cyclist's needs, since it takes only a little space in the corner of
one of the panniers, and it is light enough so that it will not drag
too much on the long hills. There are many good stoves, but the
main choice is between those fueled by white (unleaded) gasoline and those using small pressurized cannisters of propane or
butane. White gasoline is more widely available on the road, is
less expensive, and produces more heat for a given amount of
fuel than propane or butane. However, as the preceding instructions for lighting stoves should have indicated, the gasoline
stoves are somewhat more trouble to ignite.

If a gasoline stove is chosen, the Svea 123 is the runaway
winner of the commonly available models at producing maximum heat for small size and weight. The Optimus 8R and
Primus 8R are somewhat heavier, but they hold more fuel, and
their design makes them hard to tip over and easy to pack. A
fuel can will also be needed for longer trips; the flat kind with
two spouts is more efficient to use than the round bottles. The
best gasoline stove produced to date is the MSR model which
includes a pump with a small stove and draws fuel directly from
a fuel bottle of the Sigg (round aluminum) type.

There are more propane and butane stoves appearing on the

market every year. The lightest is the Gerry mini-stove, which burns butane. Unfortunately, like most other pressurized gas units, it requires its own special cartridges, and these are not readily obtainable at your friendly village general store. For this reason the stove is not to be recommended for long trips away from the supplier, since all the fuel cartridges for the trip then have to be carried from the beginning. More practical for longer trips is the Primus Grasshopper using standard propane cylinders (not the one using special butane cannisters). Since these are the same kind of cartridges used for torches, they are much easier to find along the road at hardware stores, auto supply houses, and the like, and so they are more practical for long trips than other kinds of cylinders.

Dressing on the Road and in Camp

Large wardrobes are a nuisance for the bicycle camper, increasing his load and decreasing his comfort. Naturally, the clothes that are carried have to be tailored to the weather conditions that can be expected along the route of travel. On a summer ride through Virginia, a sweater, a windbreaker, and long pants will keep the camper toasty on the coolest nights, but on a tour through the Rockies, especially in spring or fall, sub-freezing temperatures should be anticipated. A careful choice of clothing with an eye to the climate and season will be amply rewarded by comfort along the road and in camp.

For pedalling during the day, clothing which binds or chafes is a curse that can become unbearable as the miles build up. Loose-fitting or stretchy garments are essential. Shorts are far more comfortable than long pants, and they are worn by most experienced bicyclists on all but very cold days. Special cycling shorts are nice, but you can also improvise by cutting the legs off old stretch dress pants or sweatpants. (With some snaps and Velcro tape you can even make the legs you cut off into warm-up leggings, as shown in the accompanying illustration.) Whatever shorts and underwear are used, they should be tested first on a few long practice rides. Friction or misplaced seams in the crotch area or the upper thighs are unpleasant on a

Good cycling pants can be made from sweat pants. The bottoms of these were cut off to make shorts, and after hemming all the edges, Velcro strips and snaps were added, so that the legs could be re-attached for warming up in the morning, cool nights, or cold weather riding. A chamois crotch was sewn into the shorts for extra riding comfort.

one-day trip and can be incapacitating on long tours. The best cycling shorts are lined with chamois for this reason. A chamois crotch can be purchased separately and sewn into your own shorts. Adding sweatpants or windpants over the shorts makes for comfortable starts on chilly mornings and welcome warmth on cool downhill runs.

For the upper body, there are special bicycling jerseys which are pleasant, have lots of convenient pockets, and usually cost a small fortune. Just about any sort of reasonably roomy or stretchy garment will do, however, except that in heavier shirts cotton should be avoided, as it gets heavy, clammy, and cold when wet. A tee shirt, a medium weight wool shirt, and a light windbreaker make a good combination. For colder weather, a net undershirt and a sweater can be added to the outfit.

Be sure to take a knit hat. It will add more warmth than clothing anywhere else on the body. A cool cap to keep off the sun should be added for hot weather.

One change of clothes to suit the season can provide a dry outfit for camp after a sweaty day on the road, presentable town garb, and a change to use while your regular cycling outfit dries after washing. The stretchy new wash-and-wear fabrics are often very practical, since well-chosen ones look presentable even after being pulled from the pocket of a pannier, and they can be used easily for cycling in a pinch, because they don't bind. Darker hues will accept a few inevitable smears from bicycle chains and fireplaces with more grace than light colors. In warm weather a bathing suit may be the only change needed.

Rainwear

In some parts of the country and some seasons, the threat of rain can be ignored as unlikely or inconsequential. A warm afternoon shower may even be welcome after the heat of the day, and as long as the luggage is kept dry, one can simply keep pedalling. Most of the time, however, the bicycle camper cannot be so blasé; hard as it is to keep dry while pedalling a bicycle, he has to try for the sake of continued comfort.

Cyclists have a more difficult time in keeping dry than almost any other outdoor travellers. In the absence of high winds, the hiker can wear a poncho almost like a walking tent, shielded from the rain above, but with a large ventilation space below. The cyclist manufactures his own wind, and in addition he must contend with road spray from below. A cycling cape which fits over the rider, seat, and handlebars leaves the rider vulnerable to road spray and interferes with his normal view of the road. If he manages to arrange a watertight protection against all the moisture attempting to get in from the outside, he usually traps all his own perspiration and soaks himself with that.

Probably the best commercially available alternative is a rain parka together with rain pants. The seat area often gets a lot of spray when cycling, and this makes rain chaps, which are perfect for backpackers, unsatisfactory for the bicycle camper. Some pants have been made which are cut away on the sides, and these are moderately satisfactory, but it is a design hard to come by at the moment.

One solution to the rainwear problem is shown in the accompanying patterns. The large parka is cut to be very roomy, allowing reasonable evaporation of perspiration. The bottom can be left open, snugged around the waist or the waist and bicycle seat, depending on conditions. The pants use drawstrings and friction devices rather than elastic, so that the waist and cuffs can be left open when desired. When the bicycle is being ridden, the waist can be extended completely, since there is no need to hold the pants up. In fact, the same practice can be followed on the trail if suspenders are used. The cuffs will normally be closed when riding, but they can be opened in camp. The problem of wet feet is solved by the use of waterproof booties that are used only when cycling.

Sleeping Comfortably

Sleeping comfort ranks along with good food as a determinant of the pleasantness or misery of a cycle camping trip. A restful night will soothe away those tired aches in the muscles, but poor sleep just makes them that much more noticeable. Important features of the campsite have already been mentioned, but attention to the bed as part of the camp routine will be amply rewarded. The site for the tent or sleeping bag should not slope, except perhaps very slightly down towards the feet. Any other gradient, even though it seems slight on inspection, will wake you up a dozen times during the night.

Having chosen a spot, take the time to clear away all the stones, sticks, pine cones, and the like. The care needed in this operation depends on the type and thickness of the ground bed which is used, but even if cushioning is adequate, the life of the

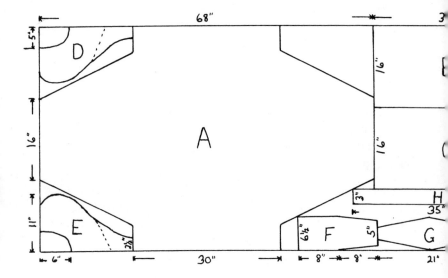

RAIN SUIT MATERIALS LIST

5 yards 44″ lightweight coated nylon fabric

1—32″ jacket zipper, double slider, separating both ends

6 drawstring clamps, spring-loaded, for cuffs and waist

6 yards drawstring (elastic may be substituted for some drawstrings if desired)

grommets and grommet-setting tool

(snaps for extra front closure optional)

INSTRUCTIONS—PATTERN—RAIN SUIT

This pattern, here cut in two to fit page space, could be laid out on any coated nylon material, but a layout is shown here for 44-45″ wide cloth. A dummy pattern should be laid out first on tissue, newspaper, or scrap material, and then be fitted. This will allow modifications to be made for individual fit before the fabric is cut. The same procedure should be followed before sewing with the cut pieces. Paper clips can be used instead of pins to avoid unnecessary holes. Remember that the fabric has two sides; the coated side should face in on the finished garment. The illustration shows two suitable types of seams that can be used.

PARKA   Sew one of the 30″ sides of B to one of the 30″ sides of A. Sew C to the opposite 30″ side of A. Now when A is folded in half on its long axis, B and C will come together. Sew one of the 16″ sides of B to the matching side of C and continue around the corner to sew two of the matching slanted sides of A together. Do the same thing to the other side of the large piece. The 16″ sides of A now form the sleeve openings and the 30″ open sides of B and C form the bottom of the parka. Cut the front opening straight up from the center of B or C to the fold in A. At right angles to this cut, make an 11″ cut in A, forming a T-shaped cut for the front zipper and head hole. Now make the hood by sewing F between D and E, the 5″ side at the front. G should be folded in half the long way and sewn around the face opening for a visor. Grommets may be inserted in the ends before sewing for later installation of a drawstring. Next, sew the hood into the head opening. It is usually best to cut the head opening out slightly with scissors to round the corners. Pin the hood in first to check the fit. The best lines for sewing it in usually follow the dotted lines in the pattern, but extra fabric is left for fit.

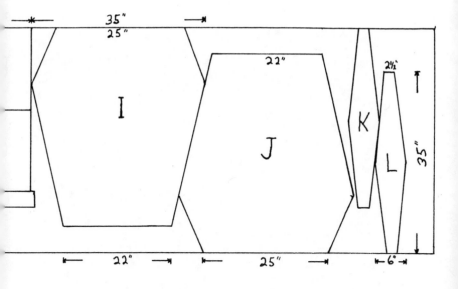

Hem both sides of the front opening. Pin in the zipper to insure proper fit. Pin H along on top of one side of the zipper as a flap to cover the zipper and prevent rain getting in. (H should be doubled with both edges tucked inside.) Sew in the zipper and the flap. Snaps may be installed to close the flap completely, if desired.

Hem the bottom of the parka and install a drawstring if it is wanted. Install elastic in sleeve ends and hem, or install grommets for drawstrings and then hem.

PANTS   Fit I and J together. Sew the two short sides of I to the matching sides of J. Now sew the two long diagonal sides of J together and the two long diagonal sides of I together. This will give the basic shape of the pants; the 22″ sides form the leg openings and the two 25″ sides together make the waist opening. K and L should be folded lengthwise and sewn on as a waistband, one on the front and one on the back. The front piece should have a grommet installed for a drawstring before they are sewn on. Install grommets or elastics in the ankles and hem.

The rainsuit shown in the patterns of this book. A long parka, rain pants, and rain booties are used.

ground cloth or the tent floor will be much longer if rough and sharp objects are cleared away before they are laid on the ground. The sleeping surface should be tested by lying down on the ground sheet or unpitched tent before further work is done. This is the easiest way to discover previously unnoticed roots, hollows, slopes, and other monsters of the night. Once the shelter, if any, is set up or a ground sheet is laid, the bed should be rolled out and sleeping bag fluffed, unless the air is especially damp. This will allow the bedding to recover from the day's packing, leaving it warmer and more comfortable at bedtime. Unless a tent is used, a separate insect bar should be set up if midnight visitors might be expected. Repellent may be adequate, but set up a bar if you aren't sure. Generally by the time bites are bad enough to wake the sleeper, they are already sufficient to guarantee several miserable wakeful hours. A bar simply consists of a large sheet of netting, weighted around the edges and held high enough at the head to prevent the bugs from standing outside while feasting on the sleeping camper.

Sleeping bags are probably the most important items of camping equipment the lightweight camper will have to consider, so they are discussed separately in the next chapter.

Ground Beds

A ground bed simply consists of an air mattress or foam pad providing insulation from the cold of the ground and padding from its bumps. Some prefer to sleep directly on the ground, but this is an inefficient way to use sleeping bag insulation. Besides this, bicycle campers these days are often forced to sleep in campgrounds consisting mainly of gravel pads designed for heavy camping vehicles, and these surfaces make for poor sleeping without a ground bed.

The choice between a foam pad and an air mattress is largely a matter of personal preference. Most people who have not become used to sleeping on air mattresses find the foam pads more comfortable. The weights of the best rubberized nylon air mattresses are comparable to those of the pads of the same size. Air mattresses pack into a smaller space, but the pads are more

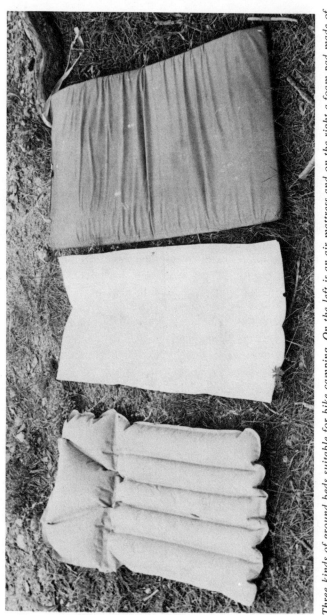

Three kinds of ground beds suitable for bike camping. On the left is an air mattress and on the right a foam pad made of urethane foam and covered with waterproof nylon fabric to keep the pad dry and protect it. In the center is a pad made of closed-cell foam (each little air pocket is completely closed off). The closed cell foam provides as much insulation as the other two types and is lighter, but it is not as soft a bed.

convenient to put out (no blowing up) and they do not spring leaks during the night. The pads are definitely warmer, and they should be chosen if this is important.

If an air mattress is taken, the cheap vinyl kinds should be avoided like the plague, since they are not all durable. Rubberized nylon is somewhat more expensive than rubberized cotton, but the difference in weight is usually worth the extra money. When the air mattress is blown up, it should not be completely inflated, since this is uncomfortable and hard on the mattress. The hips should be barely off the ground in any reclining position.

Polyurethane foam is generally best for use by bicycle campers. This type of foam has open cells, like a sponge, so to prevent moisture absorption and insure long life, the pad should be covered with fabric and the bottom fabric should be coated so that it is waterproof. Closed-cell foam provides better insulation and needs no cover, but it is not as comfortable.

Most cycle campers find that a short length air mattress or foam pad is quite adequate. It extends from the hips to the shoulders or head, and other items such as extra clothing and panniers are used to provide any necessary padding for the legs and feet.

Flashlights and Such

The camping practices of any particular group will largely determine the need for artificial light in camp. If the party rides until it is nearly dark, then it will clearly require more elaborate lighting arrangements than one making a practice of stopping in mid-afternoon. Those who get to bed early or sit up talking will not have the needs of those who like to sit up and read.

The strap-on safety light discussed and illustrated in chapter 7 will do handily for utility purposes and late night trips to the outhouse. If, however, a practice is made of getting in late and cooking or setting up a tent in the dark, it is advisable to have some kind of headlamp, which directs light where it is wanted and leaves the hands free. This arrangement is infinitely superi-

or to the practice of trying to hold a flashlight in the mouth. If riding at night is required, a battery-operated headlamp is also useful for lighting the road ahead.

The two best types of headlamps are the small French kind, which is very lightweight, but which has the disadvantage of requiring special batteries that have to be obtained where the light was purchased, and the type which uses three D cells, side-by-side. The latter kind is quite powerful and long-lasting, but it is also relatively heavy. Avoid the kind of headlamp which uses four D cells; the springs weaken, allowing the batteries to joggle and the light to flicker. Alkaline batteries are a better purchase for the camper, though they are slightly heavier than other cells and are more expensive. This is because alkaline batteries have a longer shelf life, last longer in use, especially under continuous load, and they perform better in cold weather. In cold weather, the battery pack of a headlamp should be kept in a pocket or underneath clothing since batteries operate far more efficiently if they are kept warm. If two sets of batteries are carried, they will last longer if they are switched every half-hour or so, allowing one set to rest.

Battery life depends on the size of the bulb used. A brighter bulb gives more light, but it uses up batteries faster. Batteries also have a limited shelf life, but unfortunately manufacturers are more interested in propagandizing than informing, so there is no easy way to determine the age of the batteries one is buying. The safest course is to try to buy them at a store which has a high turnover. A set which has been sitting around in a store for a couple of years (not an uncommon situation) will not last long in the field.

A lighter weight alternative to a flashlight or battery headlamp for a lot of light in camp is a carbide lamp. It uses dry fuel which gives off flammable gas when water drips into the fuel storage tank. The gas comes out through a jet in the center of a reflector, where it burns and gives off lots of light. The flame is not hot enough to present a fire hazard. The lamps can be purchased with brackets for miners' hard hats or for a special canvas cap with a bracket. With the latter it makes a fine headlamp, as well as a good reading lamp in camp. Be sure to

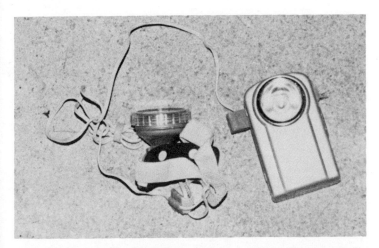

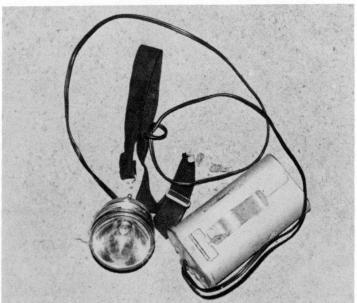

Two types of headlamps. The one on the left is a very lightweight French model which can also be used as a regular flashlight, but requires special batteries. The headlamp on the right takes four D cells and is much heavier, but it throws a very powerful beam, and batteries can be purchased anywhere.

keep all parts of the lamp clean and you will have no trouble with it. A four- or seven-inch reflector is recommended for good light output. Dust from the carbide fuel is very irritating to the eyes, so care should be taken when handling it. If you should go camping in very cold weather, remember that frozen water will incapacitate the lamp.

Spares should be carried for whatever kind of light is used, allowing both for normal use and emergencies. Flashlights and headlamps require spare batteries and a spare bulb of each type used. Carbide fuel must be carried in absolutely waterproof containers. For carbide lamps, it is a good idea to carry a spare flint and the tip cleaner, too.

Knives, Axes and Saws

A knife finds innumerable uses in living on the road, and it should be considered a basic item of equipment for any bicycle camper. However, unless one is planning on beheading an enemy or hacking through impenetrable jungle, the monstrous belt knives that are so often seen in camping stores can be dispensed with. A small pocket knife is adequate for most purposes, and if a belt knife is preferred, one with a four- or five-inch blade is plenty large enough.

More important than the size of the knife is its keenness. Dull knives are hard to use, and they are dangerous because they tend to slip off knots and other obstructions. A small pocket whetstone should be carried and used. Sharpening is really quite simple: the stone should be lubricated, and then the knife drawn across, cutting edge first, at an angle of 20-30°. Several strokes on each side of the blade, first on the coarse side of the stone, then on the fine, should do it. Stropping on a leather belt will finish the job.

Axes are rarely needed by the bicycle camper, and since they are also heavy and inconvenient to carry, there is little point in bringing one. A saw is lighter and more compact, and it will do most cutting jobs more efficiently than an axe, especially in inexperienced hands. It is only in splitting wood that the superiorities of the axe really show themselves. If a lot of splitting is anticipated, so that an axe is carried, the handle should be at least 28 inches long and the blade should be kept sharp. A dull axe is even more dangerous than a dull knife. Hatchets are much less efficient than axes, though they are nearly as heavy, so there seems little point in considering them. An axe with a lighter head, such as a Hudson's Bay style, is a better compromise, if one wants a lightweight chopping tool.

Several excellent lightweight saws are available which do a good job of cutting firewood. Several good ones weigh under a pound each and are more efficient for cutting deadfall into firewood than the much heavier, more dangerous, and more unwieldy axe.

Insect Repellents and Bars

It is normally advisable to carry a good insect repellent. Government tests have shown that diethyl toluamide is the most effective active ingredient, so the lightest weight and the best economy are achieved in products with a very high percentage. In areas where insects are very bad, an insect bar for sleeping can be formed easily with a length of lightweight nylon netting.

3

Sleeping Bags and Tents

Sleeping bag and tents are by far the most expensive items of camping equipment the touring cyclist may buy, and they can also be the most important, so they deserve special consideration. In terms of cost, weight, bulk, and influence on a trip's comfort, they loom very large indeed, and the bicycle camper should analyze his needs very carefully before going shopping for these items.

Sleeping Bags

A sleeping bag will be necessary for almost every camping cyclist from his first overnight trip, though it may well be possible to borrow or rent one at first. Since the body produces far less heat during sleep than at any other time, it needs more insulation from cool outside temperatures, unless the weather is very hot indeed. The most efficient way to provide this insulation is to carry a bag which will fit the body as closely as comfort allows.

Insulation in sleeping bags is actually provided by the tiny cells of dead air which are held by the insulating material in the bag, whether that material is synthetic fiber, foam, down, feathers, or wool. The amount of insulation is directly proportional to the thickness of the insulating layer, and is essentially independent of the material used. Thus, a down bag and a foam bag which each provide a two-inch insulation layer will be equally warm, all other things being equal. Actually there are many other complicated factors in sleeping bag design, and some of these will be considered later, but the dependence of insulating capacity on thickness is the first and most important principle of sleeping bag design. There are no miracle materials which will provide great insulation without thickness, and the buyer should be most wary of "space-age" developments. Reflective materials, for example, *will* reduce heat loss by radiation, and this is critical for an astronaut in space, where all heat transfer is by direct radiation. The camper, however, is faced with situations where direct radiation is the least significant form of heat loss and the most easily prevented. Thus, from a practical standpoint, only a very elaborate suspended baffling system could make use of reflective methods of insulation.

Since as a practical matter thickness is equivalent to insulation, materials and construction methods have to be chosen which will provide that thickness together with as many other desirable qualities as possible. These qualities include light weight, maximum compressibility so that packed bulk will be small, comfort over a wide range of temperatures, and low cost. Any sleeping bag will represent a compromise between various possible combinations of advantages and disadvantages, since no materials and construction techniques can combine all these qualities for all the possible camping situations the cyclist might meet.

Analyzing One's Needs

The first step in deciding on a sleeping bag design is to examine the conditions under which one will be camping. These depend on what part of the country is travelled, the seasons of the year when the bag may be used, and the interest of the rider in areas of extreme climate, such as the mountains. Cyclists confining their camping to the warmest months in temperate parts of the country may never meet temperatures below 50°F, while those travelling in the mountains in spring and fall have to be prepared for sub-freezing weather. The most critical condition which must be considered is the lowest temperature range the camper should reasonably expect.

This low temperature range must be judged sensibly. A sleeping bag should be adequate for comfort in any commonly occurring temperatures. At high altitude, for example, spring snows are normal well into June, and the possibility should be anticipated. On the other hand, no bag is equally suitable for cold and warm weather, so the cyclist who is most unlikely to encounter temperatures below the 40's would be foolish to buy a bag designed for high altitude use in the winter; it would be much too hot for him to ever sleep in comfort.

The second important factor to be considered in judging conditions is the upper temperature extreme under which the bag will be used. Bags designed for cold temperatures are generally not too suitable when the weather is warm, but some bags and materials are much more adaptable than others.

Finally, a number of other things influence interpretation of the temperature range in choosing a sleeping bag. Some people sleep colder than others; that is, they need far more insulation to be comfortable. Even scrupulously honest ratings by sleeping bag manufacturers can only strike some kind of average. The amount of clothing one customarily wears to bed will also be a factor. Whether a tent is used influences the amount of insulation needed in the sleeping bag, since the interior of a tent will be warmer than the surroundings. Sleepers exposed to the open night sky without the shelter of trees will radiate heat directly to the sky and will require more insulation. So will people sleeping in very windy spots, particularly without the shelter of a tent.

Sleeping Bag Materials

With some idea of his needs, the cyclist can proceed to consider available sleeping bags. Modern design has made a rather wide range of materials and construction methods available, some of them highly sophisticated. There are many excellent manufacturers with long experience in making high quality products for the lightweight camper. Unfortunately, the recent growth in popularity of cycling and backpacking has also brought a flood of shoddy merchandise onto the market.

Regardless of the insulating material used in a sleeping bag, the cover fabric should be made of nylon, which is strong, lightweight, easy to clean, and which is less prone to absorb moisture or bind. Any zippers or other hardware should be sturdy and operate smoothly. Stitching should be done well with synthetic thread. The workmanship in general should be carefully examined. Cheap bags may use a fabric with fewer threads per inch, and a starchy filler may be used to conceal the sleaziness of the cloth.

Several insulating materials are commonly used in sleeping bags. The most efficient and versatile is down from waterfowl grown in cold climates. Down is the undercoating of a bird's coat and unlike feathers, it has no quills. High quality down will occupy more volume, and thus trap more insulating air, than an equal weight of any other material. It will also compress to a smaller volume and will bounce back again and again. Finally, it allows evaporated body moisture to pass through readily. It is the best available insulating material for most lightweight sleeping bags, and hence it is used widely in the best bags. Down does have some disadvantages, however. Not only is it very expensive, itself, it requires the use of sophisticated and expensive construction methods to make effective use of its qualities. Its other major disadvantage is that if it becomes wet it collapses into a useless soggy ball.

Various synthetic fibers are frequently used to provide insulation in sleeping bags. They are generally easier to use than down, so that construction of a good bag costs less, adding to the considerable savings on material. Synthetic fibers have also been getting better and better, and for mild temperature use it is now possible to use them in making good sleeping bags for light-weight camping. Though most of the bags on the market using synthetic fibers for insulation are much too heavy and shoddily constructed, there are several good lines available. Furthermore, if a bag of this type becomes wet, twirling it around will remove much of the moisture and restore a lot of the bag's insulating properties. Still, it is important to point out that even the best synthetic insulation is half again as heavy as an equivalent amount of down and is significantly less compressible.

Foam is widely used for ground insulation either in separate pads or by inclusion in the bottom of a sleeping bag. It is also used as the insulating material in some sleeping bags. It does have some special advantages for use in boats or around the water, and it can be used effectively for homemade bags. However, it is even less efficient both in insulation per pound and in compressibility than the better synthetic fibers. At present bags made with foam are not competitive in price with comparable ones using synthetic fibers, so they do not seem worth consideration by most cyclists.

Wool is not often used as sleeping bag insulation these days, and it would not be a good material for a commercially made bag. One possible use should be mentioned, however. Cyclists camping in warm weather who cannot afford a suitable bag can use a version of the old-fashioned blanket roll. One or two wool blankets, salvaged from a chest or bought from a surplus outlet, can be sewn into a bag. An outer covering bag can be made inexpensively with waterproof fabric on the bottom and porous fabric on top. This combination will be quite comfortable in mild weather, perhaps with a foam pad or air mattress.

Sleeping Bag Design

As with materials, the most efficient construction methods for sleeping bags are generally the most expensive. For this reason, the mild weather camper does not always want to pay the premium price necessary to save those final few ounces. After analyzing his needs, the cyclist should shop widely to determine the best compromise between cost and efficiency.

Comfort may also have to be balanced against weight. A bag which closely fits the contours of the body is the most efficient, using the least amount of material to provide a given thickness of insulation and also reducing heat losses from the outer surface of the bag and from air circulation inside. Some campers find close-fitting bags too constricting and prefer a larger bag despite the extra weight. Usually, a compromise is acceptable between the closest fitting bag and the large rectangular types. Such large bags are too heavy for reasonable cycling use.

Besides general shape and materials, a great many construction details influence the warmth of a sleeping bag. Insulating material is held between the inner and outer fabric shells. With most insulators this space must be separated into many smaller compartments to prevent the insulation from shifting around. Since the insulation is compressible, these compartments should also be designed so that they allow expansion of the insulation as much as possible. This is very important with down, because it is so easily compressed. Insulation such as down is packed loose into the various compartments, while materials like Fiberfill II and Dacron 88 are used in the form of batts which may be quilted directly to material.

The easiest way to form compartments is by quilting; that is, to sew the inner and outer shells together to form pockets of appropriate size. However, the seams will be "cold seams" because there will be no insulation along them. This method of construction is therefore suitable only for relatively inexpensive bags designed for mild weather or for those intended to be used inside another bag.

A number of methods can be used to avoid such cold seams, and some are shown in the illustration. Bags made with polyester batting can use two batts sewn through from the inside and outside without overlapping, in one of the ways shown. Down and other loose fills require one of the baffling systems. The better the design of this baffling system, the more efficient (and costly) the bag will be. The thickness which results from the combination of proper materials and design is known as *loft,* a measure of the actual insulation. All other things being equal, a bag with more loft will be warmer. Caution should be used in comparing the loft

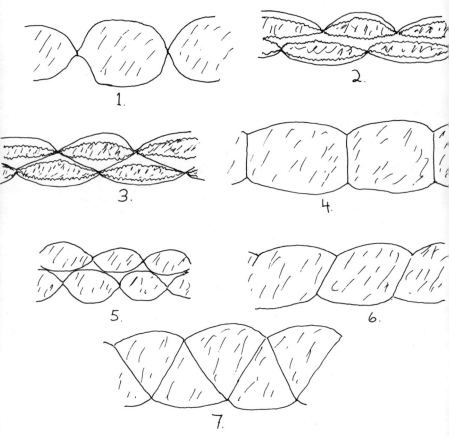

Many baffling systems may be used in the construction of sleeping bags, with the ideal being minimum weight and expense and maximum control of shifting.

1. Sewn-through construction can be used with any insulating material. It is cheap, but the cold seams make it suitable only for warm-weather bags.

2. Two polyester batts can be overlapped in this way, one sewn to the outside cover, and one attached to the inside cover, with seams offset.

3. An even better construction with batts uses a light inside layer of nylon fabric. The offset seams are sewn through the cover, batt, and inside fabric. This keeps the batts from coming apart and shifting so quickly.

4. One method of controlling down insulation is to form channels between the two shells with a very light baffling fabric.

5. A heavier and more expensive way to control the down is to have offset tubes, essentially one sleeping bag inside the other. It is very effective.

6. Slant-wall channels are a slight improvement over straight ones, since tension on one shell is less likely to compress the down.

7. The best and most expensive method of baffling is formed by triangular channels.

A typical down bag suitable for moderate to below-freezing temperatures. This one is of modified mummy design, using slant-wall baffling, and has a lightweight nylon liner to help keep the bag clean.

claimed by different manufacturers, however, since it can be measured in different ways.

Besides loft and the other features already mentioned, there should be some arrangement to prevent drafts and heat leakage along the zipper. The closure at the top of the bag should be comfortable and easily operated, and it should provide for covering the head, which is a great source of heat loss. Couples who do not choose double bags may want separate ones that will zip together. A side zipper which will open at the bottom as well as the top is useful for ventilation, particularly with bags that will be used in a wide range of temperatures.

Sleeping Bag Suggestions

The most popular bag among lightweight travellers is a medium-grade down bag of a roomy mummy design, generally using slant-wall baffling. Such a bag is good for a variety of outdoor activities, including bicycle touring when it may be undertaken in chilly weather or high altitude. On the other hand, the cycle camper who expects to be out in generally mild weather with evening temperatures rarely dropping below 40°F will probably be happier with a lighter weight bag. It will be cheaper and less damaging to his finances. On the economical side, a good polyester insulated bag with no sewn-through seams and excellent construction design, weighing under 5 pounds, can be purchased for less than $30. For a higher price one can buy a down bag suitable for the same temperatures and weighing only half as much. A versatile combination is provided by a relatively light but fully baffled down bag combined with a very light one using sewn-through seams. Either can be bought

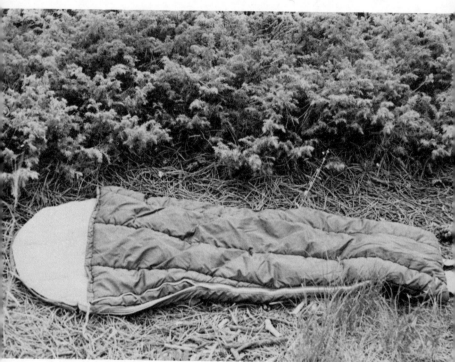

An inexpensive bag, using polyester fiberfill insulation, and suitable for camping in warm weather.

separately. The sewn-through type may be good for weather above 40 or 50°, while the other might be good to around freezing. The two together can be used for quite cold weather or for higher temperatures by people who need a lot of insulation. Buying one such bag is often the best purchase for someone working into lightweight camping, who may plan to buy the other later. Such a combination is slightly less efficient for a single temperature range than a bag designed just for that range, but it is far more versatile and allows spreading the cost of purchase as well.

Another economical possibility for those who think they need good down bags is to make a bag up from a kit. Several suppliers of such kits are listed in the appendix.

A well-made down bag is the ultimate in lightweight warmth for the self-propelled traveller, when combined with an appropriate ground bed, but it is also true that cyclists in many parts of the country do not need the ultimate in protection. Careful consideration of one's own requirements is the way to make an intelligent sleeping bag purchase.

Sleeping Bag Covers

One use of a lightweight rectangular sack, made of coated fabric on the bottom and uncoated on top, has already been mentioned, in connection with a blanket roll. Such a simple device has a multitude of uses, however, and buying or making one is strongly recommended to every bicycle camper. Such a sack provides some protection against the elements, when an imperfect shelter is used or bad weather catches the cyclist unprepared. It can also be used to extend the temperature range of any bag, making it comfortable to roughly 10° lower than it would otherwise be. Finally, the camper can sleep inside such a fabric bag on warmer nights, using the sleeping bag for a mattress or a blanket. Thus, the sack or sleeping bag cover can be used to extend the temperature range of a sleeping bag to higher temperatures as well as lower ones.

Tents

The main disadvantage to a tent as a shelter for the bicycle camper is its cost. Tents are expensive, and since it is frequently possible to do without them, other items of camping gear might be put higher on the beginner's shopping list. With all this said, however, tents still have so many special virtues that most experienced lightweight campers end up owning them. A properly made tent is durable, provides protection against insects and all sorts of weather, and allows some privacy even in crowded campgrounds.

Unless he has large amounts of money to spend, the cyclist in search of a tent should take some time at home analyzing his needs before he goes out shopping. Modern tent design has become highly sophisticated and also extremely specialized. Like any piece of equipment which will serve in many situations, a tent is a compromise. The bicycle camper has to accept this fact like everyone else, but there is no point in his putting up with a balance between the needs of high-altitude climbers in the U.S. and expedition mountaineers going to Peru. Since much of the recent work in tent design has been done with the mountaineer in mind, a great many available tents are more expensive than they have to be for the cyclist, while not really suiting his needs very well.

Thus the first step in buying or making a tent should be to list the conditions under which it will be used. If ninety percent of this use will be in warm weather, the buyer will be ill-advised to spend a lot of extra money and attach undue weight to features specifically designed for the snow-camper. On the other hand, if the tent is to be used not only for bicycle camping but also for mountaineering, ski touring, and backpacking, the purchaser will have to put up with some disadvantages resulting from the multiple uses he has in mind.

There are a rather large number of interrelated design features which the camper has to weigh against his own needs in choosing a tent, including cost, weight, packed bulk and shape, durability, wind stability, protection from insects, water tightness, condensation problems, number of possible occupants, roominess in various directions, ease in pitching, and site requirements. All these should be carefully checked and rechecked when comparing tents.

Materials

In the past few years, nylon materials have almost completely supplanted all others in quality lightweight tents. There are many good reasons for this fact, but unfortunately there are also several bad ones, having to do mostly with fashion. Since nylon is considerably stronger than cotton, it is possible to make a tent having a given amount of strength considerably lighter when nylon material is used. If this were the only result of the change, there would be no reason to lament the demise of cottons, but it isn't. To begin with, nylon costs more. It is also much more prone to produce disagreeable condensation inside than cottons, even when it is not coated. It is virtually impossible to produce a lightweight nylon fabric which is reasonably watertight but which also permits some air circulation in normal circumstances. Cotton fabric allows air to pass through and has a rougher surface than nylon, and both factors reduce condensation of moisture inside the tent due to higher internal humidity and cooler outside temperature.

Cotton and cotton-nylon mixtures thus have much to recommend them as tent materials, since they can be made quite watertight while still creating relatively little condensation inside the tent. Prolonged rain will eventually start to leak through any single-layer cotton tent, and touching the sides may start water wicking through, but these disadvantages have frequently been over-emphasized. A tent made of lightweight, tightly-woven cotton, which is well designed and waterproofed will stand up to more rain than most campers ever encounter. It is worth emphasizing here, because there has been a lot of misinformation on the subject, that condensation problems with nylon are not due only to coating. Even after being subjected to the rain so that its fibers have swollen and reduced porosity, cotton still is not as prone to condensation as nylon.

The disadvantages of nylon have been handled by a number of

design solutions. The most common is the use of a separate waterproof fly pitched over a tent made of porous nylon cloth. In effect, this is a separate tent roof pitched over the main tent. Such a fly can also be used over cotton tents to make them more weathertight and to provide extra insulation. The disadvantages of the system are extra weight, considerable extra expense, and the need for a system to pitch the fly which often adds to the expense of the tent and increases the trouble of pitching it. Other systems are also used which increase ventilation in order to combat the condensation problem. These methods eliminate the weight of the fly and its supporting apparatus, and they sometimes reduce the expense as well. Because they require positive ventilation, they are not suitable for cold weather tents, but they may suit the bicycle camper quite well.

The bicycle camper should definitely consider cotton as a possible tent fabric. He is unlikely to encounter high winds of the kind the mountaineer must frequently expect, and thus does not require the strength of nylon. In fact, proper design of stress points is even more important than fabric choice, and many of the less well-made nylon tents now appearing on the market are considerably less durable than a well-made cotton tent. Cotton-nylon mixtures can be nearly as strong as nylon, while retaining the water-resistant qualities of cotton.

Tent Design

At the moment, by far the most popular tent design is the standard mountain tent, which itself is essentially a highly sophisticated version of the old pup tent, triangular in cross-section with roughly a rectangular floor plan. Such tents may be of equal size at both ends, perhaps with two entrances, or they may taper to a smaller size toward the foot to save weight. When properly made this type of tent is nearly ideal as a mountain tent, providing excellent weather protection and good stability in high winds with a minimum of weight, but it is not a particularly roomy structure, partly because of considerations of weight and partly because of the low wind-profile needed by the mountaineer.

Though he is limited by the market (unless he wants to make his own tent) the bicycle camper should consider some of the tents

A typical tent of the two-man mountain design. This one is made of permeable nylon on top to reduce condensation, and a waterproof nylon fly is used to shed rain.

which are designed for use where weather conditions are not so severe as in the high mountains. Such tents can have steeper roofs, which allow more headroom and shed water more easily. They may have a side or a large door which can be left open for light, ventilation, and perhaps the cheer of a fire. Tent designs of this type, often known as forest tents, include the Baker, Whelen, Hill and Dale, and Forester.

Desirable Features

With any tent, the first thing the camper should look for is quality construction. Tents should be sewn with finished, felled seams. That is, the fabric edges should be completely tucked within the seam, and the fold should be shingled down so that it sheds water.

Seams are very important in tents. They are potentially weak points subject to tearing if they are poorly done, but they are very strong if well made. They are also the major point of leakage on the tent.

All points of strain for the tent, such as the spots where poles are supported, stake loops, pull-outs, guy line ties, and the like, must be reinforced to spread the strain over a wide area of fabric; otherwise they will wear through or tear out in short order. Hardware should function smoothly and be of good quality. The lines of the tent when it is set up should be smooth, not baggy. If mosquito netting is included, it must be possible to make the whole tent completely tight, including its vents, windows, door, and bottom edge. Otherwise the netting is a waste of money and weight. Regardless of the tent fabric, items like stake loops are best made of nylon, which is strong and rot-proof.

A very well-designed tent, suitable for three adults or a family of four. This tent is made entirely of nylon, with waterproof floor and fly but an uncoated roof. Three outside poles are used, between the inside roof and the fly, to save space inside the tent.

If the tent has a floor, which is a real advantage, it should be made of fairly heavy coated nylon, preferably cut so that the coated fabric extends up the sides six inches or so. This "bathtub" principle allows the tent to be pitched with slightly less concern for drainage. If a completely waterproof floor is not used, it is advisable to carry a plastic groundsheet to lay under the tent, a practice that some campers follow anyway to reduce wear on the tent and keep it cleaner and drier for packing.

Tents with arrangements for external frames are preferable to those with internal poles. They avoid the leakage problem at the top of the pole and wear on the tent floor, besides being simpler to set up. A well-designed external frame will also leave the doors of the tent clear, a matter of considerable importance with small tents.

Light weight is obviously most desirable in tents for bicycle camping, and the total weight which must be carried is what counts. Therefore, the number of stakes and poles which have to be taken should be considered, as should extras like ground cloths and mosquito bars. If the bicycle is to be covered, the weight of the cover should be counted, if another arrangement would allow the tent to cover the bike. The very best modern tents combine light weight and convenience by using an external frame which works under tension against a very few stakes, resulting in a tent requiring no guy lines and no inside poles.

Nylon tents must either be uncoated with a separate coated fly to repel the rain or must be provided with a very good ventilation system if they are made of a single layer of coated nylon. Such ventilation can be accomplished with very large side vents like those used on several economy tents patterned after conventional two-man mountain styles or it can be managed with sophisticated vent designs like those used in Jack Stephenson's tents.

Many additional convenience features can be added to tents, some of which might represent a real boon to the bicycle camper and some of which could appeal to him only if he intended to use the tent for other purposes as well. A vestibule formed in front of the door and the tent proper by an extension of the fly is often convenient for storing gear and shedding outer garments. Pockets sewn into various seams at convenient points are welcome for the storage of small items. On the other hand, zippered cook holes and frost liners merely represent added weight and expense to the cyclist who is not also a snow camper.

Recommendations

Unless the cyclist does a lot of camping in wet regions or has extra money to spend, he will probably do best to postpone purchasing a tent. In this way, he will acquire more experience and have a better idea of his real needs when he actually gets around to buying one. The virtues of a tube tent have been mentioned previously, and they should not be overlooked. Nor should those of a tarpaulin made of lightweight coated nylon. This latter

A good shelter for bicycle camping can utilize a lightweight tarpaulin with the cycle as a support. This protects both the machine and the camper. The author stakes the wheels with U-shaped stakes and uses a small loop sewn to the tarp and going around the nose of the seat, and these additions make the shelter very stable.

piece of equipment can be used in a number of ways; it is inexpensive and durable; it is lightweight and easy to set up. Altogether such a tarpaulin, pitched as shown in the photograph, is the author's favorite shelter for cycle camping. A good size is 8' x 12'. An extra loop can be placed at the correct spot on the bottom to snug around the nose of the bicycle saddle for added stability. Nine lightweight stakes are carried with it, though they are rarely all needed. A lightweight mosquito bar can be added when necessary. At least two of the stakes should be U-shaped for staking down the wheels of the cycle so that everything is completely rigid. If the cycle is taken out for a ride or an errand, the tarp is easily snugged down over everything.

The use of a tarp illustrates some of the advantages of simplicity in shelters. As tents become more sophisticated, they become better suited to special purposes, but they also get more

A single-layer tent made of cotton-nylon cloth and designed for one man. A very light and reasonably priced tent.

expensive and less adaptable to purposes for which they were not designed. For example, a sophisticated frame design allows a tent to be pitched more easily with fewer stakes and guys, but it also generally makes the tent almost impossible to pitch without the poles, meaning that their weight must always be carried and that their breakage can cause a real problem.

The least expensive reasonable alternative for the cyclist searching for a one- or two-man tent that can be used for bicycle camping and other lightweight travel is a lightweight cotton model. Slightly more expensive, but of lighter weight, are some single-layer coated nylon tents, but these should definitely be rejected if any cold-weather camping is contemplated. Finally, there are the various sophisticated backpacking tents using an uncoated tent and a coated fly, or occasionally a single layer coupled with a well-designed venting system. The smaller tents of this variety are usually roughly shaped like an A-frame or a quonset hut, while the larger ones have a central peak, giving more head room.

If the cyclist can find one of the forest-type tents of the size he needs made of lightweight material, this may be the best tent for his purposes. There have been some encouraging trends in the past few years, with some of the sophisticated manufacturers beginning to revive forest tents using modern materials and refinements.

4

Special Camping Situations

The distinguishing feature of *mountain camping* is simply that weather conditions in any particular range are likely to be more extreme, varied, and changeable than those in the surrounding country. The mountains will almost certainly be colder at night, especially if they are very high. Snowstorms will occur later in the spring and earlier in the fall. Finally, mountains generate many local winds because of differential warming and cooling, and they are likely to channel winds from large weather systems, so that gusts may reach much higher velocities than they otherwise would.

The consequences of all this for the bicycle camper are that he has to be prepared for a greater range of conditions on trips in the mountains, particularly if camping is planned at relatively high altitudes. In the U.S., there are few places in the East where severe mountain weather will be encountered along roads, except in the winter. In the Rockies and the Sierra Nevada, however, severe weather is quite common near high passes in spring and fall, and the possibility should be anticipated in summer. Conditions above timberline are always far more severe than those below.

In these situations, the bicycle camper should carry some wool clothing, make sure his sleeping bag and shelter are adequate for the circumstances, and pay attention to small details such as extra food, matches, gloves, adequate footwear for camp, and the like. When the camper is properly prepared the cool mountain nights will be very refreshing after hot days of pedalling up associated grades. On the other hand, a careless cyclist who brings little or no extra clothing may find himself suddenly placed in a very unpleasant survival situation.

Camping in Cold Weather

In general, the same sorts of cautions apply to the colder seasons as to the high mountains. Of course the crucial question is: "How cold?" Cold weather is a subjective term and will mean different things to different people and different parts of the continent. For the bicyclist, cold weather involving snow and ice is usually avoided, except on day trips. The difficulties of cycling on glazed roads are mentioned in a later chapter. Still, many very pleasant bicycle trips can be taken when the temperature at night may plunge to well below freezing. Occasionally, when the weather is good and the roads are clear, one may even go snow-camping by bicycle.

It is essential to carry adequate warm clothing when cold weather camping is planned. Wool is particularly valuable, especially for clothes that will be worn near the skin, because it does not wick moisture rapidly, and thus retains much insulating value even when wet. Cotton, on the other hand, is almost worthless as insulation when wet. For outer insulation, in jackets, for example, polyester fiber insulation is very good, since it can be dried a good deal by whipping and does not collapse when wet.

Warm hats, mittens, and footwear are essential in cold weather. A hat that will pull down in a face mask is a good idea. Mittens are warmer than gloves and should be carried even if gloves are worn some of the time. Shoes should not fit too tightly, even when worn over two pairs of heavy wool socks. Adding an extra pair of socks will not warm the feet if it cramps circulation. Wind-tight pants and parka should be carried to go over all the insulation.

Some sort of shelter will usually be necessary in cold weather, and unless something else is available, a good tent will have to be carried. Tube tents, plastic tarps, and single-layer coated tents are generally unsatisfactory in the cold.

Water may present a problem in cold weather. Streams and springs may be frozen, piped water is generally shut off, and even if snow is available it will have to be melted. The water supply should be planned ahead with these complications in mind. Extra fuel should be carried if a stove is used, particularly if snow has to be melted. Extra food should also be planned, since the body will have to burn it to keep warm.

Shorter distances should be planned in mapping out cold weather trips. Loads will be heavier, wind resistance from bulkier clothes will be greater, and the body will not normally work so efficiently. If one becomes chilled, it is important to slow down both to reduce wind chill and to avoid panting, since sucking more cold air into the lungs is not a good way to get warm.

To keep warm at night it is particularly important to sleep on a good foam pad or other insulation. If the sleeping bag is not warm enough by itself, extra clothes will help, but only if they are *dry*. Even if no real shelter is available, getting under something to avoid direct radiation to the night sky will help. Fluff the sleeping bag up well before getting in. Make sure it is sheltered from the wind. A light snack just before getting in bed helps produce heat, as do isometric exercises in bed.

Desert Camping

Desert camping is another example of a situation where extremes have to be anticipated. The advisability of choosing certain times of year for desert trips is mentioned in chapter 8. If travelling is done in fairly hot seasons, one should routinely carry a shelter which can be used for shade when necessary. A tarp, preferably light-colored for reflection, is almost ideal, since it can be pitched over the bicycle in a couple of minutes. Even when days are hot in the desert, however, the nights are often cool, so a warm sleeping bag and a few warm clothes will be needed.

Considerable thought should be given to campsites in the desert, both in advance and on the trip. Availability of water should be the first consideration, of course, since large quantities will have to be carried to a dry camp. In this respect, one cannot take chances, and one should plan on water only if one knows it is there. A shady spot is pleasant, but when the beds are put out, the angle of the morning sun should be anticipated. Unless a really early rising is wanted, a spot should be sought which will be shaded at sunrise. The morning sun rapidly makes the sleeping bag intolerable.

Arroyos, gullies, and dry washes should be avoided as campsites, since flash floods can come down very quickly indeed, often resulting from storms which are miles away. In canyons, strong local winds are common in the evening, so guy lines must be tied securely. Reasonable precautions should be taken when snakes or scorpions might be expected. One need not be paranoid in this respect, but one should not heedlessly stick his hands under large rocks, for example.

Natural water supplies in the desert should be assumed to be polluted unless one can be sure they are not, just as with other areas. One problem may be encountered in the desert that is rare elsewhere—water which is unpotable because of concentrations of salt, alkalai, or even arsenic. Local sources of information should be checked on water supplies whenever possible. In general, the absence of life around any source of water in the desert is an indication that it is poisonous. If natural water is being used, a short length of rubber surgical tubing may be useful as a straw or siphon for obtaining water from holes and tiny pools.

Camping in Wet Weather

The normal problems of protection against rain have already been discussed, but if a trip is planned in regions of very heavy rainfall, or if long runs of precipitation are encountered, a few special comments may be helpful. A good tent is definitely advisable for prolonged wet weather. Light colors like yellow make an amazing amount of difference in morale after a few days, if one is sitting out the rain. Sleeping bags and other equipment should be dried whenever the opportunity arises, even if it causes a late start on a sunny morning. In damp weather, sleeping bags should not be left out when they are not in use, but should be stuffed into a waterproof sack as soon as one gets up. Wearing wet clothing to bed only makes sense when one is quite warm and the night is reasonably dry. Otherwise, the practice will merely insure that the sleeping bag gets wet, hardly a worthwhile trade for getting the clothes a little drier and sleeping poorly in the bargain.

For extended camping in wet weather, it is usually worthwhile to carry an entire extra set of clothes apart from those used while cycling, including even extra raingear in the form of a poncho. The cycling clothes are bound to get wet during the day, between spray and perspiration, and the comfort of having a change for evening that is completely dry is worth the extra weight.

5

The Touring Bicycle

Fortunately, quite a few good books on bicycles and bicycle repair have been brought out recently, remedying the long standing lack of readily accessible information on quality bikes in this country. There is therefore no need to try to duplicate that basic information here, and this chapter will concentrate on the more specialized needs and problems of the camping and touring cyclist.

It might as well be noted that one can do some bicycle touring and camping with nearly any bicycle. There are venerable enthusiasts who swear by their one-speed tanks and manage to pedal them incredible distances. Nevertheless, one-, three-, and five-speed bicycles have real limitations for touring, especially when camping equipment is being hauled, and there are good reasons for the careful choice of equipment displayed by most experienced bicycle tourists.

The most important feature of any cycle which is to be used for extensive bicycle camping is reliability. Malfunction on a trip, especially of a kind which cannot be easily repaired, is likely to finish the tour prematurely, often for one's companions as well as oneself. Any bike being taken on a tour should be durable, well-tested, and broken-in in advance. Nearly any bicycle will develop a few problems in the first 500 miles or so, and it is best to get them taken care of where they will not cause too much inconvenience. This will also give the rider a chance to develop a feel for his machine before loading it with extra weight and to work out many necessary compromises, particularly the one between the bicycle's seat and his own.

If a heavy bike without a wide range of gears is going to be used for camping, ambitions must be kept within the range of its capacities. These will naturally vary with the terrain and rider, but they will probably be between one-half and one-tenth the distance that a rider in the same condition could expect to cover on a good ten- or fifteen-speed lightweight machine.

Quality is the key word here. In the past few years, the boom in bicycles has brought the predictable avalanche of junk cascading onto the market. Ten-speed bicycles are pouring off the assembly lines with brakes which fall apart, frames that collapse, and wheels that cannot be trued because the spoke threads strip when the nipples are tightened, to mention only a few of the problems. On a somewhat higher level, some very well-known European manufacturers are shipping bikes to this country that are put together with much poorer workmanship than the supposedly identical models they are selling in Europe. This sort of fraud will only be stopped when buyers in the U.S. demonstrate their sophistication by rejecting poorly made machines regardless of brand name.

In buying a new bike or judging the quality of an older one, there is no substitute for getting to basics. This means learning as much as possible about bikes and comparing them. One can learn a lot by reading some of the books mentioned in the appendix, by talking to knowledgeable cyclists, by looking at catalogues, by inspecting different bicycles, and by going and talking to the salesmen in different shops. Of course, many experienced people have personal biases about equipment, some justified and some not, but if the novice just keeps asking, "Why?" he will soon begin to separate the wheat from the chaff.

Looking at a Bicycle Critically

The first rule to remember in judging bikes these days is to avoid depending on little giveaway code signs which used to be considered as indicators of quality. Center-pull brakes are found on very good bikes and on some of the most appalling pieces of junk on the market. By the same token side-pulls are put on some of the less expensive bikes of reasonable quality, some of really poor manufacture, and on some of the best hand-made machines available. There are now a number of good manufacturers of high-quality tubing, but one can no longer assume that really good tubing indicates a really good frame. Labor costs and demand have gone up, and there are now some rather poor frames being made even from double-butted Reynolds 531. Let the buyer beware!

The frame is the critical part of any bike, especially of a touring bike that is expected to carry a load of camping gear over bumpy roads, preferably with a minimum expenditure of effort by the rider. If a prospective buyer doesn't like the brand of brakes which come with a particular bike, he can easily have a different kind put on, usually at nominal cost. Even if the decision is made after the bike has been used for a while, accessories are relatively inexpensive to change. The frame, however, is the most basic part of the bike; it is the most expensive part and determines the major handling characteristics, durability, and overall value of the machine. The best accessories in the world will not give a poorly-made frame the feel of a fine bicycle.

Since this is the case, one should practice looking at frames carefully. Materials *are* important, and any decent bike has to be made of high quality seamless lightweight alloy tubing. The best ones use butted tubing, at least for the main triangle, which means that the tubes are thicker at the ends where they must take the most strain and thinner in the middle where the load is lighter. If you are looking at bikes in shops, ask the salesman about the tubing. If you are looking at your own bike or a second-hand one, there may be a label somewhere on the frame which will tell you what kind of tubing is used. Finally, of course, what counts is the way the frame feels when it is ridden, but even this takes some practice to feel at first. Some idea of the resilience of the frame can be gotten by holding the bike tilting away by the handlebars and seat while pushing gently against the end of the crank axle with the toe. It is pretty easy to feel the difference between a heavy dull frame and a nice resilient one this way.

Proper constructions of the joints of the frame is at least as important as the materials used. Most well-made frames and many poorly made ones use lugs at the tube junctures, but some very good frames are made with lugless joints. Examples of both types are shown in the photograph. Whichever method is used, the joints should be brazed at a fairly low temperature, never welded. The quality of the brazing at the lugs will tell a lot about the skill of the frame-maker and the workmanship of the frame. Ideally, the brazing alloy should form a smooth, continuous bond along the joint of the lug and the tube or the two tubes. Unfilled spaces and blobs of brazing alloy are signs of sloppy construction, while perfectly finished lugs are the hallmark of a master framebuilder. Any good frame will have smooth and workmanlike joints, though the difference from the very best frames is apparent to a practiced eye. On a bike which has been ridden for a while, the imperfections in the finishing of joints will be apparent on inspection, because the little crannies which are formed collect road dirt and are difficult to clean out.

Third on the list of vital frame characteristics is alignment. The frame has to be true; that is, each tube must be oriented properly with respect to the others. Any misalignment will insure that the bicycle will never handle properly. Later compensating adjustments on wheels and other parts of the bike will not be able to make up for misalignment of the frame, and under a load of camping gear, the resulting problems will only be accentuated. There are many ways to measure a frame to check for misalignment. The simplest series of tests I have seen is suggested in *Bike Tripping*.

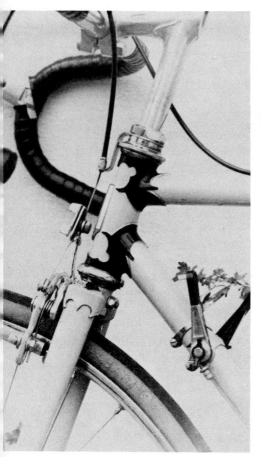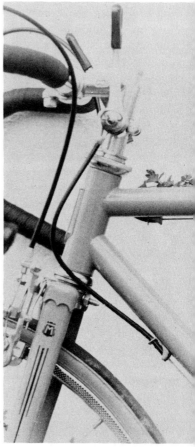

The headsets of two bicycles. The one on the left is a lugged frame, that is, special joints are used into which the tubes fit, before they are brazed together. The right-hand frame uses unlugged construction, in which the tubes are held by a jig while brazing. Most better bikes use lugged frames, but unlugged ones can be satisfactory as long as they are brazed, not welded. The left-hand photo shows center-pull brakes and the right-hand one side-pull brakes. The low mounting of the shift levers, as in the left-hand picture, is generally preferable to stem mounting.

Beyond the characteristics just mentioned, which hold for all frames, the individual is faced with the choice of a frame with particular characteristics. The feel and performance of the frame are influenced by materials and proper construction and by the choices made concerning dimensions and proportions of the frame. Those interested in technical descriptions of the frame-builder's art are referred to the books mentioned in the appendix. In general, a frame ideally designed for bicycle camping will tend to be longer and more flexible than one intended for most other purposes. These terms have a rather flexible meaning, however—a frame that will feel stiff to a lightweight and easy-going rider may seem very limber to a heavier, stronger one. The characteristics desirable for bike camping are achieved by decreasing head and seat angles and increasing fork rake and chainstay length. For those not particularly concerned with such technical considerations, however, it is quite reasonable to forget about dimensions and concentrate on the feel of a bike. A knowledgeable dealer will be able to sort out technical matters, anyway.

One dimension the cyclist *should* pay attention to is the length of the seat tube from the center of the bottom bracket to the opening at the top into which the seat post is inserted. This dimension is also known as the *size,* and is the one which is critical if a bike is to fit the rider. Most people get bikes which are too large for them to ride properly. For a first crude idea of size, straddle the bike with your feet on the ground, as shown in the illustration. The crotch should clear the seat tube enough to allow standing comfortably with the bike straight up. If the bike has to be tilted it will require awkward maneuvers for mounting and stopping, which are especially inadvisable on a bike which will be carrying luggage. For a touring bike, the tube should not be too much lower than necessary for the crotch to clear comfortably, because a smaller frame will result in lower handlebars, an advantage for the racer but not for the tourist, who often likes to cruise along with a fairly high handlebar position.

For a more precise determination of frame size, measurements should be made as shown in the illustrations. These may be particularly necessary if a bicycle is special-ordered. For custom-made bicycles, different frame-makers have their own methods for

Checking a bike for size. The rider should be able to straddle the frame comfortably with feet flat on the ground, but ideally the touring frame should not be smaller than necessary.

measuring an individual, but the frame size measurement is fairly standard. Using the method of measurement shown, the largest frame that an individual can ride properly will be the one which has that measurement from the top of the pedal to the top of the seat, with the seat all the way down. Any larger frame would force him to extend his toe farther, reducing pedalling pressure, or to slide back and forth on the seat, which would cut his tours very short indeed. This largest frame size would be determined as follows:

> Largest possible frame size = leg measurement shown + ½ pedal thickness - crank length - height of seat in lowest position.

Normally, 170 millimeter cranks are used by the tourist, approximately 6¾". Height of the seat at the lowest position is usually 2½", and the pedal thickness changes the distance by about ½". The cyclist can check to see if these figures apply; if they do:

Largest possible frame size = leg measurement - 8¾"

This size frame is usually a little too high to straddle comfortably, and a better frame size will be about two inches smaller.

Proper frame size = leg measurement - 10¾"

There is some leeway in size, and the cyclist will be able to ride a frame two or three inches smaller quite comfortably, but the larger size is probably best for touring, so long as it can be comfortably straddled.

Gear Ratios and Equipment for Camping and Touring

There seems to be a general mystique surrounding the subject of gearing systems, an aura of mystery and status that is both confusing and silly. Actually, both the gearing and gear-changing systems of the ten- and fifteen-speed machines designed for camping and touring are extremely simple, far simpler than those of three-speed hub bicycles, for example.

All modern bicycles use a direct chain drive to transmit force from the pedal cranks to the axle of the rear wheel. The chain itself runs between a toothed gear or sprocket attached to the crank axle and one attached to the axle of the rear wheel. Though many other drive systems have been conceived at one time or another, this simple method has always proved to be the most efficient available. The number of turns made by the rear wheel for each revolution of the pedals and cranks is dependent on the number of teeth on each sprocket. If the same number of teeth were present on each, the rear wheel would turn once for each turn of the crank; if twice as many teeth are present on the crank sprocket, the rear wheel will go around twice as many times as the pedals are turned, and so forth.

People's legs, like most sources of power, can work best when they are operating at a certain speed range against a certain amount of resistance. In other words, the amount of work done in getting the cyclist and his load up a hill is the same regardless of the gear, but some gears make the job much simpler for the body. A car will go up some hills very easily and smoothly in first gear, while in second gear the engine strains most inefficiently and barely makes the climb, and in third gear the car would stall and never get up at all. The human engine works in an even narrower range—if the gear is too high, the human engine stalls or at least is strained beyond reasonable capacity. A gearing system changes the distance travelled by the bicycle for each turn of the pedals, and thus changes the effort required for each turn of the pedals. Ideally, with an appropriate set of gears, the cyclist will be able to continue to turn the pedals at the same rate all the time. When he goes uphill or fights a strong wind, he will use a lower gear, and when the going is easy he will use a high gear, but the pedalling tempo and resistance against which he is pushing will remain relatively constant.

A little thought about these requirements will make it apparent that there is no one answer to gearing problems. An ideal range of gears will allow the cyclist to pedal at his most efficient level in all conditions he might meet, including pedalling up the steepest hills with the heaviest loads, against the strongest winds he might meet, and down the fastest runs he may encounter. Also ideally, he should have closely spaced gears throughout this range, so that he can choose the most efficient ratio in any given situation. Finally, the gears should be easily shifted and operate smoothly in all ratios. Proper ratios will depend not only on objective conditions, such as the grades of hills that exist in the area of travel, but also on the physical condition, training, and cycling style of the individual rider.

In addition to all the ideal specifications mentioned above, however, choice of gears also depends on the designs available and their limitations. Touring machines suitable for the wide variety of conditions to be found in North America have used the extremely simple idea of derailing mechanisms in order to change from one gear to another. There have been recent developments which may ultimately result in other mechanisms being used, but for the time being, derailing shifters, generally known by their French name, *derailleurs,* are likely to remain standard for some while.

Derailleurs are simply gadgets which are used to move the drive chain from one gear to another by pushing it from side to side. Gears attached to both the pedal cranks and the rear axle are mounted side-by-side in what is known as a *cluster,* and derailleurs fixed at appropriate places along the length of the chain force it in the direction of the desired gear. Details of the specific workings of particular changers can be found in the repair manuals mentioned in the appendix, but they are really fairly simple.

Two main design problems arise in the derailleur system of gear-shifting. The first arises from combining a chain drive with side-by-side sprockets. A chain works very efficiently when it travels along a straight path between the driving and driven gears, but it begins to develop a great deal of friction and strain if it must travel at an angle. Naturally, the derailleur system depends on moving the chain in such a way that it operates at various angles. The larger the clusters at the front and back, the greater the angles of deviation will be in some of the gear combinations. The practical consequence of these factors is that gear clusters larger than two on the cranking axle and five on the rear wheel axle begin to cause serious difficulties. Clusters larger than three on the front and six on the rear are completely impractical.

One of the reasons that the ten-speed arrangement, consisting of a rear cluster of five with two sprockets in front, is so common is that larger numbers of gear combinations require excessive chain angles. Even the ten-speed has only eight combinations, since the two combinations requiring maximum chain angles should not be used. They tend to put too much strain on changing mechanisms and usually overlap in the gear ranges they provide.

Cleaning the freewheel cluster. Regular maintenance is essential for the proper functioning of a camping bicycle, and it also familiarizes the tourist with his machine.

The other major problem which arises in designing derailleur systems is that different gear combinations require different chain lengths. The old one-speed Huffy you may have had as a child had only one sprocket in front and one in back, so the chain could run between the two with very little slack, and thus with little power loss. Since a set of front and rear clusters require widely varying chain lengths, there has to be a slack piece of chain in some gear combinations, and there must also be an arrangement to take up the slack and pay it out. This is handled with an extra spring-loaded take-up wheel on the rear derailleur, but because of the mechanical problems this causes, the designers of changing mechanisms make their devices to take up only what they feel is essential. Since many of the best derailleurs are made with the needs of road racers in mind, they have only the capacity needed for the very narrow range of gears that these racers use.

The upshot of all this is that in choosing gears, the camping cyclist must keep in mind not only the range that would be desirable for his body but also the limitations of the mechanical gear changing systems used on modern cycles and the capacity of the particular equipment he may want to use. The problems of fifteen and eighteen speed systems are such that it is advisable to avoid them completely, unless the extra range they provide is essential. Similarly, very wide ranges between gears in the front and rear clusters will also require a large capacity in the changer for taking up slack chain, and this will limit the choice of changers, possibly even requiring special modifications.

The actual gear range required will depend both on the kinds of touring one is planning and on the physical condition of the rider. For general touring and camping in moderately hilly regions, it should be possible for nearly any rider to use a ten-speed selection of gears and obtain an adequate range for all normal conditions. If tours with heavy loads in mountainous areas are contemplated, some riders may wish to include a third sprocket on the front cluster to provide a very low hill-climbing gear, but the disadvantages of this system should be recognized. The author has toured in the Rockies successfully using a ten-speed system consisting of front sprockets having 52 and 40 teeth and rear cluster with 14, 17, 20, 24 and 28 tooth gears. A somewhat lower range could be obtained without spreading too much by reducing the front sprocket sizes, perhaps to a 36 and a 50. Unless the tourist is a very strong rider indeed, he should avoid the close ratios designed for the racer. The author's personal preference is to avoid three-sprocket front chainwheels because of the excessive angles that are produced, but it should be noted that many experienced bicycle campers do prefer this combination.

Whatever gear ratios are chosen, the touring cyclist should try to use good equipment. Bicycle camping puts a good deal of strain on the drive chain, and poorly made components will often cause trouble at very inopportune times. If a bicycle is being bought specially for touring, negotiations for equipment changes should be undertaken at the time of purchase, both because new equipment trade-in value is naturally higher and because the buyer has more leverage. A dealer may be willing to make some exchanges at cost in order to sell the bike, and his labor charges will nearly always be less. Special attention should be given to the capacity of the rear derailleur. The advertised capacities are usually a good deal higher than the equipment can handle without considerable strain, and the bicycle camper should make his choice in a range well below this maximum. Special attention should be given to testing this part of the bike. If the derailleur does not function smoothly when it is brand-new, perfectly adjusted, and free of road dirt, it will cause nothing but trouble out on the road.

A word about discussions elsewhere of gears, ratios, and the like: the analysis here is relatively brief because there is plenty of information elsewhere for the interested reader and because too much attention is often paid to the subject. The final combination of gears and changes has to shift smoothly, be appropriate to the rider's demands and physical condition, and should provide a fairly smooth transition from one gear to the next, so that rhythm is not broken each time the gears are changed. A rider in good condition will choose fairly narrow ratios for many types of riding, while a novice is more likely to need a wide range. The ranges suggested above would be appropriate for a novice in average riding, but they are good for an experienced rider carrying heavy loads of camping gear, particularly over a lot of hilly ground. For the novice carrying a lot of gear, I would recommend smaller chainwheels, giving lower gears, but maintaining the same sort of range. I feel this is a better solution than using very wide ranges and imposing the attendant strain on equipment. As with other bicycling problems there are many other good solutions, and experienced cyclists will argue for hours over gear combinations.

If this sort of thing is appealing, the beginner should understand the meaning of gear charts. A final gear is usually expressed in the distance in inches travelled by a bicycle for each revolution of the crankshaft. Thus, a one-hundred inch gear is one which makes the bicycle travel one-hundred inches each time the pedals make a complete revolution. This is dependent on wheel size and the ratio of the front and rear sprockets. It is sometimes called the "gear ratio", though this is a misnomer. Thus, a 54-inch gear would be produced by many possible combinations. With the common 27-inch wheel, for example, it would be the result of a 56-tooth chainwheel and a 28-tooth rear sprocket, and of 52-26, 50-25, 48-24, 46-23, 44-22, 42-21, 40-20, 38-19, 36-18, and so on. In other words: any 2-1 gear ratio on a bike with 27-inch wheels will give a 54-inch gear.

Tires

Another major decision which must be made by the purchaser of a bicycle for camping is the type of tire to be used. Brands and weights of tires can be changed quite easily at any time, of course, but because the two major types of tires use different wheel rims, a choice between them must be made when the bicycle is purchased, unless the cyclist takes the rather expensive course of having his wheels rebuilt at a later date or getting two complete sets of hubs, spokes, and rims.

The choice between the two major varieties of tires is not easy, but the advantages of each are quite clear, so the decision is not nearly so complicated as the choice of gears. "Sew-ups" or "tubulars" are generally lighter and will accommodate higher inflation pressures and thus produce less road friction. Lighter weight is of particular importance in tires. The tire travels farther than the main part of a bicycle and develops angular momentum as well as the momentum along the path travelled by the cycle, so much more work is done to propel the weight of the tires than to push along weight in the frame. Thus, saving a few ounces in the tires counts for much more in terms of effort saved than lopping off a few ounces anywhere else. Similarly, avoiding a little extra road friction can make a great deal of difference. The other main type of tire, variously known as the "clincher", the "wire-on", and "tube-type" tire, is generally heavier and will not take as much air pressure as the sew-up kind. It is, however, cheaper and usually more rugged and durable than the sew-up.

There are a number of qualifications and subtleties in the choice of tires, but these are really fairly easy to understand. To begin with, there is a bit of confusion which often arises in the minds of beginners over the ease of repairing damage to the two kinds of tires. Tubulars (sew-ups) are preferred by road racers partly because they are very easy to change. The tubular tire is complete, and the innertube inside is completely enclosed by the tire, with the whole thing held on the rim by air pressure and a bit of glue. When air pressure is removed, the whole tire can be peeled off quite easily and another tire can be put on and inflated by an experienced cyclist in a matter of a minute or two. A thorough job using new glue or glue-impregnated tape takes a little longer but is still very quick. In addition, this is a very practical matter, because sew-ups can be folded into light and compact packages, so that several can be carried very easily.

There is a catch, however. Sew-ups, though they are very easy to *change,* are a confounded nuisance to *repair.* Even after one has acquired a good bit of experience, quite a lot of time and patience are required for the simplest repairs on sew-ups, while repairing a clincher is rather simple. Clinchers are built the way car tires are, with two wire bands holding the tire on the rim. Inside this outer tire, as with some car tires, are innertubes which actually hold the pressurized air filling the tire. Since the wires retaining the tires on the rim must withstand this air pressure, the amount of pressure is somewhat limited, and the difficulty in removing the tires from the rims is increased, particularly since great care has to be exercised to avoid deforming the rims. Thus, though clinchers are much easier to *repair* than sew-ups, because the tubes are readily accessible, they are somewhat harder to *change.*

Actually, the speed of tire changing is of interest mainly to racers and people interested in some sort of record. What mainly concerns the bicycle camper on an extended tour is the total time required to take care of the damage caused by a puncture, and there is no doubt that sew-ups are far more demanding in this respect. Sew-ups are just what their name implies. The outer casing is sewn together to completely encase the inner tube, and to gain access to any portion of that tube to make repairs, the stitching must be cut and later re-sewn, a process sometimes further complicated by the difficulty of being sure just where the puncture took place.

The cycle camper weighing advantages should therefore award clinchers a clear decision in terms of convenience of repair. Clinchers are also much more resistant to puncture than are sew-ups, and they have the additional advantage that when one is riding in those parts of the country (especially the Southwest) where thorns are a special problem, heavier duty "thornproof" tubes can be installed until the danger is past. Clinchers are also more widely available than are tubulars, which can be an important consideration on long trips. They have always been considerably cheaper, and this difference is becoming more and more significant, since the price of sew-ups has been going up at an astronomical rate recently.

On the opposite side, though the lightest clinchers approach the weight of the heavier sew-ups, the latter still have a very strong advantage in terms of weight and rolling resistance. Spare sew-ups are easy to carry, and though spare tubes are easy to carry for clinchers and are usually all that is needed, spare tires of the wired-on variety are quite cumbersome because of the stiff rim cables. Finally, though sew-ups are fragile in their resistance to punctures, the author has found good ones to be just as tough as clinchers in their durability under general road shocks.

In general, clinchers seem to have the clear advantage for the bicycle camper unless he is devoted enough to sit out in front of his tent at night repairing his sew-ups. Some enthusiasts may be willing to put up with this inconvenience for the slight edge in performance that tubulars will provide, but most cycle campers will be far happier with wired-on tires, the best of which are quite light and will withstand considerable pressure.

Directions for actually fixing tires are fairly simple for clinchers and rather complicated for sew-ups. Both are adequately covered in repair manuals and in the directions that come with patching kits. A bicycle patching kit of the appropriate type should be carried, since it will be lighter than one designed for cars, and car tire patches are too thick even for clincher tubes. Sew-ups require special kits with thinner patches, thread, etc. A few points may be helpful:

- With sew-ups it is more convenient to carry pre-glued cotton tape for gluing tires back on the rim; it is less messy to handle than glue.

- With clinchers, it is essential to carry a pair of bicycle tire irons to initially pull the bead over the rim. Improvising with screwdrivers will guarantee wrecked rims. Whenever possible, the hands should be used to push the bead on and off the rim to avoid damage.

- With either type of tire, the puncturing object will usually remain in the casing and must be removed when the hole is found. With clinchers, a mark should be made on the tire to correspond with the valve stem in the tube, in order to facilitate locating the object once the hole is found. Otherwise, the tire is likely to be rotated around the rim so that it is impossible to find what the original position was.

- A slow leak often means that the tire is punctured and a thorn or splinter is still sticking through the casing and tube. The tire should not be deflated until one is ready to make repairs, because if the air is let out and then the tire is blown up again, the tube will often slip off the original hole, the thorn will make a new puncture, and the original puncture will change from a slow leak to a fast one.

Proper care of tires is very important if they are to have long life and if constant repairs are to be avoided. One should get in the habit of checking tire pressure with the thumb whenever one mounts the bicycle. Riding with underinflated tires will quickly ruin the casings, and will leave both the tires and the rims vulnerable to damage from all sorts of road hazards. Overinflation, though less common, can cause blowouts or can unseat the bead of a clincher from the rim. The cyclist has to learn to keep an educated eye on the road ahead, watching for patches of broken glass, potholes, and other hazards. Tire-savers, little wire gadgets that skim along the tread of the tires to pick out imbedded material, are a real help, particularly with sew-ups. Alternatively, one can allow the palm of a glove to ride along the top of each tire occasionally, particularly after encountering glass fragments and the like.

Clincher users may want to investigate "cheaters", which are special very light and flexible wire-on tires using standard innertubes and clincher rims. They are new and very hard to find, but they have some special advantages that make the effort worthwhile. As shown in the illustration they can be folded almost as well as sew-ups, so they are easy to carry as spares. They are also light enough so that they should perform nearly as well as sew-ups for fast running on good roads.

The user of clinchers must also decide which of two types of valves he should buy. Innertubes can be purchased either with the valves used on car tires (Schraeder) or those used on

Spares for the clincher user: a "cheater" wire-on tire and an innertube.

sew-ups (Presta). Those with Schraeder valves are more general-ly available and can be filled directly with gas station hoses. On the other hand, the best bicycle pumps are usually fitted for Presta valves.

An increasingly annoying problem for cyclists is the deterio-rating quality of tires in general. The rubber in tires requires considerable aging if good wearing qualities are to be obtained. Despite greatly increasing costs, virtually all available tires now being sold are "green" and deteriorate rapidly in use. This can be very costly, especially when sew-ups are used, and it also creates real supply problems for anyone taking very long camping tours when tires wear out prematurely. Little can be done on a short term basis by the individual rider, but buying tires a year or two in advance of use is a wise investment.

Cranks and Pedals

Better bicycles have special alloy cranks and pedals to reduce weight, but some well-made, less expensive machines use steel for the purpose. The method of attachment of the cranks to the cranking axle is of some importance. The best cranks are the cotterless variety; a square hole in the crank fits exactly over a square-ended axle and is held on by some sort of recessed bolt. The cottered cranks used on cheaper cycles use a special flat-sided cotter pin mating with a flat surface on one side of the crank. Cotterless cranks have a special advantage for the cycle camper, because they can usually be properly removed and in-stalled with an easily portable tool. Cotters need to be pressed in and out, and this can often cause real problems if maintenance is needed along the road. Both cottered and cotterless cranks should be periodically checked for tightness, particularly with a new bike or after reassembly. Loose connections can cause deformation of the fittings and require new cranks or axles, particularly with soft (and expensive) alloy cotterless cranks.

Various experienced cyclists have different preferences for crank length, depending on riding style, leg length, and bicycle design; 170 millimeter cranks are fairly standard and seem to do a creditable job for most riders. Longer cranks give greater leverage and thus require slightly less force to push, but they will also require the legs to travel a greater distance and may be more tiring in the long run. Longer cranks, together with a large drop (the distance down from the line between the axles to the center of the bottom bracket) may cause the pedals to hit if they are turned during cornering. In general, the tourist should stick to cranks between 165 and 175 millimeters unless he has special reasons to deviate.

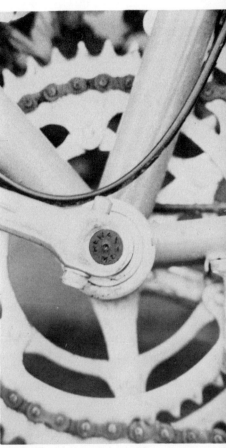

On the left is a cotterless crank and a lugged bottom bracket; on the right is a cottered crank and an unlugged frame.

There are lots of good pedals around, the main criterion being that they operate smoothly. The bicycle camper should choose some sort of "rat-trap" pedal—the kind that has teeth along the front and back to grip the shoes, usually includes a little raised cage on the outside to keep the feet from slipping that way, and has provisions for attaching toe clips and straps. Coupled with the right sort of shoe, such pedals enable the cyclist to clamp his feet into the pedals so that he can transfer energy to them with minimum wasted effort.

Hubs, Wheels, and Bottom Brackets

One of the really convenient innovations made in the last few years has been the introduction of sealed hubs and, more recently, bottom brackets. On long tours, particularly in wet or dusty conditions, conventional hubs must often be torn down for cleaning and greasing. This requires carrying necessary tools and is often quite inconvenient on the road. Modern sealed bearing units offer high performance components which are maintenance free for years of heavy use, and they are well worth the extra initial investment, particularly for the touring cyclist. One caution: like any other component, sealed bearing units should be well-tested on rides close to home before taking off on an extended trip. A criticism that might be levelled at sealed bearing units is that parts, servicing, and tools for handling them are likely to be much harder to find than for more conventional equipment.

Whether sealed or unsealed bearings are used in the hubs and bottom bracket, good quality and good maintenance are vital. These bearings are the main running and load-bearing ones on the bicycle, and their smoothness of operation is vital to that of the whole machine. Any of the well-manufactured brands on the market will do the job, but only if they are properly maintained. Except for the sealed types, bearing sets need to be periodically disassembled, cleaned, regreased, and adjusted. Methods for doing this are simple enough for anyone who is mechanically inclined and has the proper tools, and one of the repair manuals mentioned in the appendix will help those who want an introduction. Cleanliness is vital to the proper maintenance of bearings. All the old grease and grit has to be removed before regreasing and reassembly. The frequency of need for repacking will vary greatly with conditions of use. In riding conditions that are dry and not too dusty, bearings will only need attention once every six months, or so. If a great deal of riding is done, or if one rides a lot in the rain or on dirt roads, the bearings will need attention more often, sometimes as often as once a week—any stiffness, noise or irregularities in the operation of a bearing indicates that it needs attention.

The best hubs are made from lightweight alloys. They come in two main styles, high flange and low flange. The high flange hubs project further, so that a shorter distance needs to be covered by the spokes, and they are generally used to provide more rigid wheels. This is not particularly desirable in a camping and touring bike, and low flange hubs are recommended. Quick release hubs are nice and are included on most good bikes these days, but they aren't essential. Avoid wing nuts on the rear wheel; they can't be tightened sufficiently without using a wrench.

The wheel is built out from the hub. Spokes should be butted (thicker at the ends) and laced. Laced spokes are crossed so that they touch at the outermost intersections; this helps to distribute road shocks and makes for a more rigid wheel. Spokes can be crossed-over-three or crossed-over-four; in both cases the term refers to the number of other spokes crossed by any given one between the hub and the rim. Spokes crossed-over-four give a more rigid wheel, but they tend to break more easily. Standard wheels have 36 spokes, but 40 are sometimes used for a stronger rear wheel. The rear wheel has to be dished, that is, the spokes on the sprocket side have to be shorter, giving a flatter pattern to make room for the sprocket cluster. Naturally, the wheels must be true, but there is bound to be a good deal of shifting and stretching in the first few hundred miles on a new wheel, and retrueing will be necessary. Some cyclists like their spokes tied together with wire at the outer intersections and then soldered, giving a more rigid wheel that stays true longer. This should not be done until the wheel has been ridden for some time and retrued.

Most experienced cyclists pick light alloy rims, though they are more expensive and delicate than stainless steel. The spoke holes should be reinforced with ferrules for strength. The rim must be of the proper type—designed for either sew-ups or clinchers.

The left-hand photo shows a quick release clamping mechanism on a rear hub and a high quality forged fork-end. The right-hand picture shows a standard nut used with a stamped fork-end, which is normal with less expensive bicycles.

Brakes

Most of the brakes used on decent bicycles are quite adequate if they are kept properly adjusted. Both side-pull and center-pull brakes have their advocates, but a lot of the choice comes down to expense. There are quite a few cheap side-pulls around that don't work very well, but recently center-pulls have started to appear that are just as bad. Generally, good brakes in the medium price range are center-pull, because it is harder to make good side pulls. Snobbery and dogma will do no good here, though, because the best brakes made (and the most expensive) are side-pulls. The best thing for the shopper to do is to test the brakes. Be particularly wary about the return. Most brake problems arise when the brakes stick *on,* so be sure that yours return easily. If they have a tendency to stick when they are new and clean, they will probably always stick when they pick up a little road grit to add friction. Excess friction is usually in the cable system.

The major considerations of proper operation and release are of the most importance for any cyclist choosing brakes, but there are a few other items worth watching. Alloy parts are as effective and much lighter than steel. If the tops of the handles are wide, they are more comfortable to lean on, and rubber hoods make them even better. Quick releases, on the brakes, in the cable train, or on the handles, make removing the wheels much simpler. Ease in adjustment is a real help, particularly with adjusters placed on the handles where they can be set while riding. Well-finished brakes are a lot easier to clean. Brakes that squeal loudly are often annoying.

Brakes should be adjusted so that the pads move straight in against the rims. If they hit the tires, they will cause trouble. There should be a minimum of slack travel, so the cables have to be kept tight with the pads just far enough away from the rim to avoid any rubbing. Adjusting the pads so that the front ends hit the rims just ahead of the rear ones will sometimes cure squealing.

Tandems require more stopping power than caliper brakes on two wheels can provide, and they usually have a hub coaster or disk brake on the rear wheel. Some cycle campers who carry heavy loads also like to add these to normal cycles, and they do have particular advantages in wet weather. Reasonably conservative riding on steep hills seems to work equally well, however, and is much more effective than special brakes in avoiding skids on gravel and wet pavement.

A lot of touring cyclists like extension brake handles that can be used when riding on top of the bars. This is largely a matter of personal preference, but anyone using the extensions should recognize their limitations. They do not provide nearly as much leverage as the regular hand grips, and many of them are dangerously weak.

Seats and Handlebars

Seats for touring long distances have to be narrow to avoid interfering with the legs. Seats that are wide at the back are intended for an upright sitting position for pedalling around town. They look comfortable, but on long trips they cause far more seat pain than they alleviate. Padding is a matter of personal preference, but the seat should be very smooth. The legs will go up and down 60 to 100 times per minute for quite a few hours on a long trip, and a little friction each time will add up to very sore skin by the end of the day.

Some of the new plastic seats are very good, and they are preferred by quite a few cyclists. A good butt leather seat is heavier, more expensive, and takes longer to break in, but it will eventually mold itself to fit the rider, if he survives the experience, and sweat has less of a tendency to collect between the leather seat and the rider.

Anyone who wants to enjoy long bicycle camping trips should ride on a new saddle quite a bit before going on extended tour. There is a process of accommodation which has to go on between a new saddle and the rider's anatomy which is best undertaken on day trips. It is a difficult period, but as long as it seems possible that the rider may win the battle, he should persevere. Once the saddle (or the rider) is properly broken-in, it is best to keep that saddle, regardless of the number of bikes it moves to. This is particularly true of a well-made leather saddle which has been broken-in to fit the rider. It is a truly priceless possession, as anyone who has just come in from a hundred miles on a new saddle will attest.

The touring cyclists puts a lot of his weight on his hands, so the handlebars are important to him, both because they provide support and because they determine the position of the rest of the body. They should allow a wide variety of different positions to accommodate different sorts of pedalling that may be encountered during the day and to allow different muscle groups to be rested by shifting position. Fortunately, the shapes of the bars put on most decent cycles sold in this country are fairly well adapted to the needs of the cycle camper. For light weight, the bars are best made of aluminum alloy. One good design has a wide, straight, horizontal section before the bars bend forward and then down, a style shown in the illustration. Perhaps even better is the uncommon style which bends upward before going forward and down. This enables the cyclist to ride higher when he wants to, either for resting or standing up in the saddle when pushing a load up a steep hill. The bars should turn downward, since the lower, streamlined riding position is very efficient and frequently used. The style which begins turning down immediately should be avoided, however, since it makes all the higher riding positions uncomfortable and is designed mainly for racing.

To try out a set of handlebars, the frame size should be correct and the seat set at the right height. With the hands on the lower part of the bars, the rider should be streamlined and able to use the muscles in the torso to put power into his pedalling, but he should not feel cramped. The highest position should be restful and allow the abdominal muscles to rest and the neck to unkink. These positions can be adjusted somewhat by changing the length of the stem extension, changing the height that the stem protrudes from the head tube, tilting the handlebars, and moving the seat forward or back. All these adjustments are limited, however. The tip of the seat should be between 1½ and 3 inches behind the center of the crank axle and the stem has to go at least a couple of inches into the tube below for safety. The length of the stem extension is fixed, so if a different length is needed, that should be determined before buying the bicycle. With everything adjusted the bars can be tried out properly, and cyclists who find that the highest position available on standard bends is still a little low can try a pair with an upward curve.

Whatever style handlebars are chosen, the beginning tourer should take off the tape and experiment with different brake positions. The bars can be retaped, starting from the middle. Many bicycle campers like to pad the bars under the tape to give extra protection to the hands against road shock. Some people wrap cotton fabric tape underneath; some use foam rubber. I like the method suggested by Richard Jow in *Bicycling!,* using rubber from an automobile inner tube and then wrapping with twill tape.

Accessories For the Camping Bicycle

Fenders   Many bicycle tourists and campers use fenders to help provide protection from rain and mud, both for the rider and the machine, but because of their extra weight they are not used by others. The choice is perhaps best made on the basis of the weather in the area where one is touring. Fenders and associated paraphernalia have little place in the southwestern deserts, but they make quite a bit of sense on the Gaspé Peninsula. If riding is done in rainy areas without fenders, clothing needs to be more effective if one is to stay even tolerably dry. Aluminum fenders are often used, but plastic fenders are somewhat lighter, even though they are less durable. Mud skirts can be used for extra protection, as can a mud flap on the front wheel to protect the feet.

Lights   Several considerations should go into the choice of lights. For the cycle camper, they should serve the dual purpose of working in camp as well as on the road. Styles of touring must be considered in evaluating the likelihood of night riding. Some provisions should always be made for riding in the dark in case of emergency or unforseen problems, but more elaborate measures would normally be used if one is planning on long days that may frequently stretch out into dusk.

For riding, there are two distinct uses for lights; the first allowing the bicyclist to see the road ahead and the second to make him visible to passing motorists. The second is by far the more important. Much of this purpose can be served by judicious use of reflectors, reflective tape, and bright clothing.

The best riding light is the strap-on type shown in the illustration in Chapter 8, which shows red to the rear and white to the front and doubles as a reflector even if the batteries die. The major advantage of the strap-on light besides its light weight is that when attached to the leg or the ankle or just below the knee, its motion attracts the attention of a motorist at a much greater distance than a steady lamp fastened to the bicycle. Even though a driver has no idea what the light is, he will usually see it bobbing up and down on the cyclist's leg, while any stationary light of a practical size will often escape his attention until the last second. This type of light will also serve quite well for camping, unless one habitually does a great many chores after dark; it can be strapped on an arm to leave the hands free when one is occasionally caught washing dishes or pitching a tent at night.

The strap-on light is only marginally effective for the other riding purpose mentioned above, that of enabling the cyclist to see the road ahead. Really good visibility is just about impossible at night, but those who claim that a front light is unnecessary for night riding must have confined their cycling to populated areas with street lights or to moonlit nights. Riding down a dark country road at night without a light can be really scary; it is not only impossible to see potholes and obstacles, often one cannot even stay on the road. The strap-on light will do as an emergency device for those who don't expect to actually be caught out at nightfall, but those with ambitious itineraries may feel the need of something more adequate. Probably the best solution is a headlamp with a separate battery pack. It is very useful in camp, and since it is never attached to the bicycle, it doesn't have to be put on or removed. The beam is not fixed in its angle from the handlebars; it goes wherever one is looking, whether it is well ahead to see the direction of the road or just in front of the wheel to catch the details of a chuckhole. It can also be quickly waggled in the direction of a motorist coming from a side road, who will frequently not see a bicycle headlight pointing straight ahead. One type of headlamp is shown in the illustration which throws a very powerful beam. A very small lightweight French model sold in a number of mountaineering shops is excellent, except that it takes an unusual battery, so that one could not purchase refills along the road.

Rain Covers   When travelling in wet areas it is wise to carry a rain shelter for the bike; after it has faithfully carried the cyclist through the day, it is ungenerous to leave the poor machine out in the rain. Leaving the bike unprotected is also a lot more work, since the bearings will have to be disassembled and greased a lot more often. Even if the cycle is ridden in the rain, it makes sense to get it out of the weather whenever it isn't actually being used. One can buy a plastic rain cover meant to fit the bike, purchase or make a permanent coated nylon cover, or just buy a sheet of plastic the right size and carry a few spring-loaded clothespins to seal the ends.

Pumps   A pump is essential for the bicycle camper. Fixing a flat does little good unless the tire can be reinflated, and even finding the hole will probably be impossible unless a pump is carried. Most cheap pumps and some expensive ones will not bring the tire pressure over 40 pounds or so, enough to allow one to walk the bike to a gas station, but not to ride it. A really good pump is a better idea, but unfortunately most good pumps are made to fit Presta valves. If one of these is purchased, the cyclist will have to buy tubes using Prestas or find an adapter going from Presta to Schraeder.

Shoes and Cleats   Whatever is worn around camp, shoes for riding must be reasonably light and flexible and have sturdy soles. Light-soled sneakers will not protect the feet from the pedals. Lightweight hiking shoes with lug soles will often serve very well both for riding and camp, if grooves are cut in the soles to exactly match the lines of teeth in the pedals.

The best shoes for riding are special cycling shoes. These should have cleats attached as shown, so that the shoe fits the

Proper fitting of a cleat to a bicycle shoe. The cleat should be fitted so that when the shoe is locked onto the pedal with the strap, it is absolutely straight. If the cleat, and hence the shoe, is offset, power will be lost.

toe clip and is exactly parallel to the crank. If the cleats are not aligned properly, pedalling will be inefficient. The shanks that are nailed onto the shoes should be the long steel kind. Plastic and aluminum cleats are designed strictly for racing and are easily broken.

Cleats allow maximum transfer of power to the pedals, so special cleated shoes are recommended, but since they can't be worn around camp, extra shoes have to be carried.

Locks and Chains   The problem of securing the bicycle is sometimes much less pressing for the bicycle camper than for the city cyclist, but it can be much more acute. Good bicycles are becoming more expensive and more marketable every year. In some parts of the country a token locking system to discourage juveniles is still quite adequate, but in an increasing number of places, bike thievery has become a well-organized professional operation. Cycle campers spend most of their time on their bikes, and night spots are often secluded enough that one can sleep near the unsecured cycle without too much worry. The problem is that even one occasion requiring the bike to be left unattended in a vulnerable spot necessitates locking it properly.

Campers travelling in groups are quite a bit better off on this score, since on most occasions one person can stay with the bikes. When many stops in dangerous spots are anticipated, a group can carry a couple of really adequate chains and locks to handle quite a few cycles, thus reducing extra weight to a reasonable figure. Lengths can be determined beforehand.

The lone cyclist has the worst problem, having no one to watch his bike and being stuck with the entire weight of any locking system he carries. In some cases a bit of bravado will provide a much lighter substitute for a hardened chain. One can carry the bike into the occasional restaurant or rest room, request the local gendarmes to allow one to park it in the police station, or use one's ingenuity in a variety of similar ways. Hiding the bicycle may also work in some cases. Bicycle shops or local cyclists are usually sympathetic and willing to help.

A lightweight and simple locking method will often serve the camper's purposes, discouraging casual thieves. For example, it may be possible to leave the bicycle in an attended spot, like the office of a gas station, where the attendant would be able to guard against theft by someone equipped with a chain cutter or hacksaw, but may not be able to keep constant watch. For such purposes, a light cable with a small tumbler lock will usually suffice without adding too much to the tourist's load.

Unfortunately, for any kind of reasonable security in more hostile environments, like big cities and college towns, one has to put up with rather heavy chains and locks, and these may have to be carried. If the bike is to be left for any length of time at all, the chain should have links at least 9/32 of an inch thick, and should be of hardened steel made for this purpose. Chains that aren't hardened are easy to cut, and if they are hardened too much, they can be shattered with a hammer. Cables don't offer as much security for the weight. With proper locking technique, the camping cyclist may be able to get by with two to two and a half feet of chain. The method is to remove the front wheel and then run the chain through the rear triangle and the front wheel. The lock to go with it should be a tumbler lock with a hardened hasp, preferably one that latches on both sides. (The hasp will be labelled "hardened", and will have notches on each end where it snaps into the case.)

Chains made for locking bicycles usually come with plastic sleeves to protect the bike's finish, but a length of discarded innertube will substitute nicely. A chain of the sort described with lock and sheath will weigh around two pounds.

Repairs and Maintenance on the Road

This is not a repair manual, and this book would have to be doubled in size to cover the subject of repairs completely. Bicycles are fairly simple precision machines, however, and there are several good repair manuals described in the appendix at the back of the book. Any serious bicycle camper ought to learn as much as possible about making repairs so that he will be prepared for trouble on the road. The best way to learn to fix a bike is to do most of the work it needs on a day-to-day basis, a procedure which has the extra virtues of keeping the bike in good shape, saving mechanic's charges, and enabling one to accumulate the tools needed for the work.

Several items ought to be obtained when the bike is purchased, if at all possible. They will be needed later and will probably be a lot easier to get if they are purchased with the bike, besides, the buyer is in a better bargaining position when buying the bike. I recommend getting the following spare and special tools with the bike, aside from other items mentioned later:

> extra axle nut (if the bike has them)
> extra spring for quick release hubs (if the bike has them)
> freewheel remover to fit your freewheel
> several extra spokes of each length used in your wheels, labelled (there may be as many as three different lengths)
> crank tool (if you have cotterless cranks)
> extra cotter (if you have cottered cranks)
> several extra bearings for hubs, headset, bottom bracket, pedals (possibly two sizes), and derailleur wheels (if used)

If the bicycle dealer doesn't know what length spokes were used in building the wheels or what size bearings are used in something, he ought to be able to find out. He will certainly be more able and willing when he is trying to sell the bike than six months later.

As noted above, maintaining one's own bike is probably the best way to learn the basics that are needed to make repairs on the road. As one works on the bike, it is a good idea to keep notes on a piece of paper that can be carried in the tool bag. Lots of small bits of information can be very useful when one is making a repair or hunting for a part in a strange area. The dimensions of spokes, size and make of components, number and size of ball bearings are useful things to know. Check the threading of your freewheel; there are two major types, and they aren't interchangeable. This way, if you have to phone around a strange city looking for a part, you'll know exactly what you need.

Tool and repair kits will vary a good deal, depending on one's bike, on the sort of trip, and also on the problems that have come

Using a chain tool to open a chain, a necessary step if the chain is dirty enough to require soaking. Regular maintenance of touring bikes is essential to avoid unnecessary problems on the road.

up in the past. Each cyclist is usually prepared for the repair that came up on the last trip. On most trips one should be equipped for the common problems: lubrication, broken cables, broken spokes, flat tires, and worn-out brake pads. Bicycles are pretty durable, trouble-free machines if they are kept in good running order, and one should not have to anticipate major repairs unless one is on an endurance trip on the Baja Peninsula, or some similar rough and remote region. Obviously, if one starts a trip with worn-out components or crashes the bike, a lightweight repair kit may be inadequate.

The following suggested kit is on the comprehensive side, and not all these items will always need to be carried. Clearly, a group can also avoid carrying duplicates of many parts, where they are

One method of carrying spare spokes so they will always be with the bike. The top of the plastic bag can be tied to the frame of the seat after the spokes are inserted all the way into the tube.

interchangeable, though each member should be able to handle small problems like flat tires. One useful practice is to have a small tool pouch which is carried on all trips and another with the additional items needed for longer jaunts. If everything is kept in two nylon ditty bags, packing is speeded up and essential items are less likely to be left behind.

> patching kit (correct type for sew-ups or clinchers)
> 2 tire irons (for clinchers)
> 1 or more spare clincher tubes or sew-up tires
> spare clincher tire (rarely needed)
> tiny crescent wrench
> small crescent wrench (about 6"; jaws should be narrow to remove pedals)
> hex keys required by particular bike
> lightweight screwdrivers, as required by bike
> 2 or more extra spokes of each size used
> cotterless crank tool
> chain tool
> spoke wrench
> freewheel remover
> tire pump
> 2 or more brake pads
> spare derailleur cable
> spare brake cable
> spare cross cable (for center-pull brakes)
> 2 spare ball bearings of each size used in bike (in small plastic tube)
> small can of chain lubricant
> small container of bicycle grease (Lubriplate is good, Phil Wood is best)
> rag and tube of hand cleaner

Clearly, many of these items will not be necessary on all trips, but one should be sure to carry the things that are. A derailleur cable weighs very little, and carrying one is far preferable to pedalling a hundred miles in high gear over hilly country. (Moving the stop screw to fix the bike in a lower gear is an

A method of hanging the cycle for repairs or maintenance in the field. Parachute cord is used to form two loops hung from a tree branch. One hooks under the handlebar clamp and the other goes around the seat. Spare spokes are shown here wrapped in a plastic bag and attached to the pump.

improvised solution.) Any particular bike may not need some of these items and may require a few special ones; this is what one finds out by doing maintenance work ahead of time. Several situations would also require borrowing extra tools from a mechanic. The freewheel remover cannot be used without a big wrench, but the wrench can be borrowed from an auto shop.

Repairs that can be handled on the road are limited by the rider's mechanical experience and talent, by his tool kit, and by the circumstances. Foresight is the most important ingredient in handling road problems successfully. If one is planning a lot of travel on rough roads, he should plan on more flats and

broken spokes. If maintenance problems are allowed to accumulate before a trip, they will almost certainly cause trouble.
Frozen bolts and worn bearings should be worked on at home
near a bicycle shop, not out in the boondocks.

Broken Spokes

One repair problem deserves some special attention. As has already been mentioned, spare spokes should be carried for each
length used in the wheels. Replacing them is normally simple
enough. The broken ones are removed, new ones are inserted with
care to match the wheel pattern, and the wheel is trued by alterna-
tely tightening the new spokes until the rim comes into line. It is
usually best to remove the tire first, even if the old spoke nipples
are not frozen, so that the new spoke end facing the tire can be
flattened down if there is any protrusion. Spare nipples should be
carried, since the old ones are often impossible to unscrew.

The difficulty arises when the broken spokes are on the
freewheel side of the rear wheel. Examination will convince the
novice that it is impossible to insert a standard spoke without
removing the freewheel. Even though a freewheel tool is carried,
this operation requires a vise or a large wrench, and spokes are
not always sufficiently cooperative in choosing a time to break.

Probably the best solution to this problem is to have a hub
specially drilled on the freewheel side so that each spoke socket is
keyhole-shaped and the spokes can be inserted without removing
the freewheel. Such hubs are hard to get, however, and another
solution is to have some extra spokes that are specially bent and
have the right length to be used temporarily. The exact method
will be dependent on the lacing of a particular wheel, but an example is shown in the photograph of the method used successfully
by the author.

Transporting the Bicycle

On camping trips which begin at some point far from his
home, the cyclist's major problem is often how to get his

A technique for temporary repair of a broken spoke is shown. A spoke slightly longer than the one to be replaced is bent into a sharp U at the opposite end from the thread, in such a way that when hooked in the junction between the hub and the first spoke crossed, the threads of the bent spoke reach to ¼" short of those of the spoke to be replaced. In the photo, a replacement spoke is shown running parallel to the spoke it would replace. When a spoke is actually broken, it can be removed, and the bent spoke inserted, the bend tightened, the nipple tightened, and the wheel trued. The arrow shows the bent end of the spoke and the X indicates the one to be replaced.

bicycle to or from the touring route. Most commonly, the bicycle is carried by automobile, though it may occasionally be taken on an airplane, bus, or train. The lone cyclist can frequently simply remove one or both of the wheels from his bike and put it in the back of the car, but this is not always convenient, and if more than two people have to be carried with their machines, it is generally impossible. In these situations, the bicycles normally have to be carried on the outside of the car.

A typical bumper rack holding two bicycles.

The most important requirement for any automobile bicycle rack is that it be rigid and sturdy enough to hold the cycles mounted on it with complete security, though many other features are desirable. The rack should hold the cycle in such a way that the finish is not marred or accessories damaged. Obviously, if the rack is to be used for more than one bike, they must not bang against one another, and it is more convenient if the rack is designed so that a lot of padding does not have to be added. Convenience is obviously desirable for bike racks, though it must sometimes be weighed against expense. Some racks are much simpler for loading and unloading bikes than others, though this may concern commuters more than campers. The ease of putting the rack on or removing it is often just as important, as is the interference it may cause with access to the trunk or engine compartment.

The major advantages of rear (and front) racks are that they allow easy loading and removal of the bikes, and that less wind resistance results from carrying them in the low positions. On the other hand, bikes carried on those racks are more vulnerable to road dirt and to damage by other vehicles. Many bumper racks are not sturdy enough or are badly designed, and they often interfere with the trunk or with the engine compartment. At the very least, the rack should be firm, and the bikes should be carried completely above the bumper so that bouncing cannot drag them on the road. Some excellent racks are now being made which can easily be removed, but they will not fit all cars.

Top racks usually are easier to make in such a way that they will fit most cars, that they will carry more than one or two bikes, and that they will hold those bikes solidly without allowing the bikes to bang against one another. Further, the cycles are carried in a place where they are out of the way and are better protected from road dirt and damage. A roof rack is also often easily adapted for other uses, such as carrying skis, canoes, or kayaks. The disadvantages of top racks are that they normally make loading and unloading the bikes somewhat more difficult, that considerable wind resistance is usually added by top loading, and that top loaded bikes are subject to damage from low branches, garage doors, and the like, if the driver should be careless.

It is practically impossible to make recommendations on particular racks since possibilities, advantages, and disadvantages are dependent on individual circumstances. A rack which is made for a Volkswagen bug may not fit any other car, and the needs of a person who carries the bike only for a few camping tours each year are quite different from those of the man who uses both auto and bicycle for a daily commuting trip. It is worth mentioning that separate gutter brackets are available for use in homemade roof racks, and that such racks are readily adaptable to different automobiles and different needs.

For transporting bikes on public transportation, it is hard to make definite recommendations. The cyclist will find that usually the best tactic is to assume (or act as though he assumes) that the bike will be allowed as a piece of luggage. Public transportation companies should be pressured to install appropriate carrying racks, but in the meantime it seems wisest to get a bicycle carton and pack the bike. This doesn't take long and provides sure protection. Some experienced air travellers simply turn the handlebars, reverse the pedals, and put protective padding on the derailleur. They do not put the bikes in cartons, but do take the precaution of carrying them down to the plane themselves.

On Amtrack trains there is now a special rate of $2 to take your bike along to your destination. In some cities free cartons are even available.

6

Loading the Bike

Safety and enjoyment of bicycle camping are greatly enhanced by loading the bike properly. It is, of course, quite possible to cycle along with a sixty-pound load carried on the back in a rucksack or a packframe, but this is a terribly inefficient, uncomfortable, gruelling, and unsafe way to go. The cyclist with a backpack has to work against his load, holding it up while trying to pedal, and at the same time fighting the bicycle, which has been made unstable by the high placement of a heavy load.

The basic principles for loading the bicycle are these:

1. Keep the load light.

This is the hardest rule to follow, but it is one of the two most important. Heavy loads are a drag to haul, they put excessive strain on many parts of the bike, making breakdowns in awkward places far more likely; they make the whole system less stable, especially on downhill runs, they decrease the efficiency of the braking system, and ninety-five percent of the time they are just plain silly.

2. Reduce bulk as much as possible.

It is almost as much of an enemy as extra weight. Bulky items are difficult to pack and hard to keep stable on the bike. They increase wind resistance, making pedalling and steering much harder than they would otherwise be.

3. Keep the load low down.

The lower the weight on the bicycle, the more stable, safe, and easy to ride it will be. This is the main reason for the use of panniers, rather than other loading arrangements. The panniers hang down beside the wheels, so that the load is kept low on the bike. In keeping with the same principle, heavier objects should be packed low in the panniers when possible, rather than being put up on the carrier or in the handlebar bag.

4. Balance the load.

In order for cycling to be efficient, as much power as possible has to go into the pedals, rather than being used up in a fight with balancing and steering problems. Safety is also dependent on proper balancing. The need for side-to-side equilibrium is fairly obvious and simple. When loaded, the bicycle should stand straight up while held with only a light touch. The front and back loading also needs attention, however, in order to maintain good handling characteristics. The rule of thumb is that 45% of the weight should be on the front wheel and 55% on the rear. Depending on the total weight being carried, the rider may prefer to put up to two-thirds of the weight on the rear, but less than one-third of the weight on the front wheel is likely to make the bike unstable on downhill runs. Front-to-rear balancing will be approximate anyway, since the bicycle camper is unlikely to carry around a scale to measure the load on each wheel. Bulk should be concentrated in the rear, however, with lightweight but bulky items like sleeping bags usually loaded on the top of the rear carrier.

A properly packed bicycle. Rear panniers, a handlebar bag, and a sleeping bag stuff sack carry all equipment. The load is distributed between the front and back wheels. Heavy items are kept low, and the whole is firmly fastened. Three stakes and a short length of parachute cord hold the bicycle upright.

Nearly all the practical tricks to loading a bicycle for camping follow from these rules, together with a few other fairly obvious principles such as the convenience of having frequently used items packed where they are easy to get and the necessity of having the load stay put on the bicycle rather than swaying ominously on corners or falling off after a bump.

Carriers

In order to carry packs large enough for camping equipment, the bicycle needs special carriers which will hold the packs where they will fit and transfer their weight to the wheels or to sections of the frame strong enough to carry them. The standard types are carriers fitting over the front and rear wheels and those designed to hold a handlebar pack away from the bars, so that the hands are still free to use any position. The rear carrier is a necessity, since rear panniers will be needed even with the lightest weight camping equipment. There are a number of good carriers around, but the availability of particular ones will depend on suppliers and local shops. The most important features are light weight, strength, and rigidity when attached to the bicycle. Numerous convenient points for attaching clips, ties, and hooks are helpful. Clearly, the carrier must fit the bike on which it will be used—this should not be taken for granted, especially by people with center-pull brakes. Avoid rear carriers that are supported by brackets going to the seat stays; they always slip.

A pack carried on the handlebars generally requires a frame also, unless it has one built in. If it is used to carry more than a few pounds without a frame it usually has to be strapped tightly to the handlebars to keep the pack from flopping, and this interferes with the hands on upper parts of the bars. Several frames and brackets for front packs are available to solve this problem.

Usually, on moderate trips it is possible to carry all the necessary equipment without a front pannier rack. Loads should be kept between twenty and thirty pounds, perhaps even less. It is quite possible to manage this even on very long trips, providing occasional points of resupply are available along the way and special circumstances do not intervene. If, on the other hand, a trip is being made in really remote parts, requiring carrying food for a couple of weeks, water for several days, or special equipment, loads may creep up to forty or fifty pounds. In a similar situation are parents carrying both children and camping gear or strong cyclists carrying much of the equipment for weaker members of the party.

With larger loads like those mentioned above, a rack should be obtained which will carry a set of panniers over the front wheel. Such racks are common in Europe, but they tend to be rather hard to get in the U.S.

One of several types of carriers for handlebar bags. This one is easily removed when it is not needed. Like any good rack of this kind, it holds the bag clear of the bars so that the hands can be used in any position, and keeps it well away from the wheel.

Packs for Bicycles

Panniers are the standard bicycle packs. They are borrowed from animal packing, and unfortunately too many of those on the market never got redesigned on their way from the horse or the mule to the bicycle. Panniers are two packs which hang on either side of the carrier, sometimes connected by fabric in between, and sometimes separated, using some sort of direct connections to hang from the carrier. They may include an accessory compartment fitting on top of the luggage rack.

The most important features of panniers are the fixtures that attach them to the carrier. A sloppy arrangement which allows them to slide around in any direction is all the hint the prospective cycle camper should need to look elsewhere. Such arrangements guarantee an unstable bike, rapid wear on the pack itself as the fabric rubs back and forth, and excessive strain on the parts of the bike. Finally, any pack which is improperly designed in its connections to the carrier is almost certainly badly thought out in other respects as well.

The next thing that the cyclist should check is the way the pack fits his bicycle, himself, and his riding style. Even an excellent pack may not fit all carriers or bicycles. Ideally, the carrier and panniers or saddlebags should be bought at the same time, unless the camper is making his own pack. Attachments must be positive. The pack, *when loaded,* must have good clearance with all moving parts, including the cyclist's feet. Apparently, some packs have been made to fit bicycles which are only ridden downhill, since they are made without adequate clearance for the heels. Even well-made packs, however, may not clear on some frames, since clearances depend on foot size, chainstay, crank, and other lengths, and on individual riding style.

All saddlebags or panniers should be waterproof and be made with reasonably sturdy materials and construction methods. They should not have a tendency to bulge into the moving parts of the cycle when they are stuffed, and stiffeners or metal stays are used to prevent this and to lend stability to the pack.

Numerous pockets and compartments which are easily reached are a convenience when one is looking for a particular item, and they aid packing by preventing things from shifting around. There should not be so many compartments that one cannot easily pack larger items like cook sets, however.

There are all sorts of convenience features that can be built into panniers and saddlebags. Lots of zippered pockets are very nice to help in finding items when they are needed. So are attachment methods which make it easy to get the bags on and off the bike and tie-in points for attaching extra gear easily. On panniers there may be arrangements for fastening the two together for easy carrying and for fastening one or both to a packframe for backpacking. With either saddlebags or panniers, it's nice to have convenient carrying straps for hauling the packs in camp. Such extra frills are often expensive though, and should never take precedence over essential features: durability, positive attachment to the bicycle, weathertight construction, fit and clearance from moving parts, and carrying space.

Front packs should have similar characteristics to rear ones, with the same factors having priority. Closures which are easy to open and placed in convenient spots deserve more consideration on the handlebar pack, because this is usually where items used during the day are carried. It's very useful to be able to pull out a handful of nuts or stuff in a hat while riding. A transparent, waterproof map compartment on the top is convenient, making routefinding at road junctions and planning stops much simpler. This pack should not be loaded too heavily, however, lest the weight throw balance and steering off. If a heavy load is being carried, so that a lot of weight needs to go over the front wheel, front panniers will be needed; they bring the load lower down, and their carrier transfers most of the weight directly to the axle without loading the headset and the fork.

Front panniers or saddlebags should meet exactly the same criteria as the rear ones, except that they will be smaller and shaped differently. To try them, load them up, and then ride the bicycle slowly around a lot of sharp turns, making sure the panniers don't interfere with turning.

Small packs are often carried on the back of the seat, and these are very useful for packing miscellaneous items, providing they don't interfere with normal loading of the carrier. Many bicycle campers don't use them because they interfere with strapping a sleeping bag atop the rear carrier.

Stuff sacks, though not packs in a strict sense, are very useful to the touring cyclist. Small stuff sacks will serve to separate items inside the panniers, so that they can easily be found, especially if the panniers are not well supplied with pockets. Thus, cooking odds and ends can be kept in one bag, necessities for personal hygiene in another, and so on. Stuff sacks are also used for packing compressible items like down clothing into a small space. Finally, larger stuff sacks for sleeping bags and tents are often strapped directly to the top of a carrier, leaving the panniers for smaller and heavier equipment. Stuff sacks for use outside other packs should be made of sturdy, waterproof material, or they should be supplemented with heavy duty plastic bags.

Miscellaneous Carrying

A number of items are usually attached to the bicycle by means of special brackets in various spots. These include the tire pump, water bottles, tool kits, and spare sew-up tires or clincher innertubes. When there is room available, the cyclist can easily make similar arrangements for some items like fishing poles, tent poles, camera tripods and the like. Such things can often be carried on the inside of the frame triangle, providing they are short and thin enough. Elastic straps or spring clips serve as fastenings which are easily undone, or parachute cord can be used.

The recommendation has already been made that backpacks be avoided for general use on the road, though some experienced cyclists carry a few light items in a small day pack. There are some situations in which a pack is useful in bicycle camping, as for hauling water and food obtained a few miles away from camp. For this purpose, a very light frameless pack is best; it can be rolled up and tied onto the frame. Improvised packs like those shown in the illustration will even serve the purpose. If the

A pack can easily be improvised for carrying groceries or water. This one is made from a pair of rain pants. The legs of the pants pass under the cyclist's arms and are tied to the waistband. Stuff sacks also make handy improvised packs.

pack is intended for backpacking trips from a roadhead along the way, a frame pack may be preferred, and the cyclist will have to put up with the inconvenience of a frame tied to the top of his carrier. The author uses a sturdy and well-designed frameless pack for this purpose to avoid the annoyances presented by carrying a frame pack on a bike.

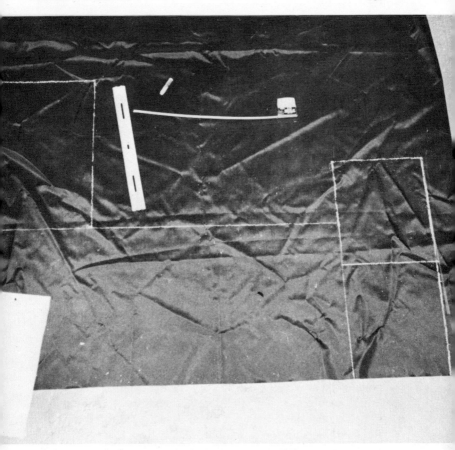

Laying out a pattern, using chalk and careful measurements.

If cameras, binoculars, or other such items are carried on the body, it is a good idea to provide them with wider straps than normal for the sake of comfort. A chest harness is particularly useful for heavier cameras to prevent their damage and the annoyance of their constant bouncing and the continual need for adjusting their position.

Patterns

Patterns are included here for rear panniers and a front bag. They are fairly detailed and should not be too hard to follow, either with a sewing machine or hand stitching. Still, a few cautions are in order. Coated fabric is advised, and any stitching which is later pulled out will leave a line of holes. It is recommended that a dummy pattern first be laid out, cut, and pinned together, using paper or scrap cloth. Any mistakes can then be corrected before the cutting and sewing is done on expensive fabric. It must also be remembered that most waterproof fabrics are coated on only one side; this should generally face inward on the finished pack, so that the coating will be protected from abrasion.

Dummies or measurements should be carefully checked against the bicycle and carrier that the bags are to fit. One of the advantages of making your own packs is a custom fit, but it is important to remember to actually do the custom fitting, especially when fastening hardware is put on.

Carrying Children

There are quite a few bicycle carriers made for children, but none of them is really satisfactory for the camper. The obvious initial requirements of light weight and sturdiness eliminate most carriers on the market out of hand, since they are either flimsy or weigh a ton, often both. Recently a few good carriers have appeared which use molded plastic seats, but what is really needed is a lightweight rear carrier which will also allow small panniers to be carried behind the child's legs. This is particularly true because the extra clothing needed for small children will add considerable bulk to the packs, even though the added weight is small.

If one is shopping for a commercially-made carrier, a third requirement should be added to those mentioned above. Guards are needed to prevent the child's feet from getting into any moving parts, particularly the spokes. For the most common carrier position, with the child sitting behind the saddle and fac-

Sewing a bicycle pack. A simple seam is being used here, simply sewing the two pieces together ½″ in from the edges. A second seam is then sewn inside the first to back it up. Note that the sewing is done on what will be the inside of the pack. The coated side of the fabric faces in.

Sewing the straps on a handlebar pack. Snaps or other fixtures are first put on the strap, and it is then sewn with several lines of stitching. All points of strain, as at the ends, should be reinforced with several lines of stitching. Fancy machines are not necessary, as can be seen here.

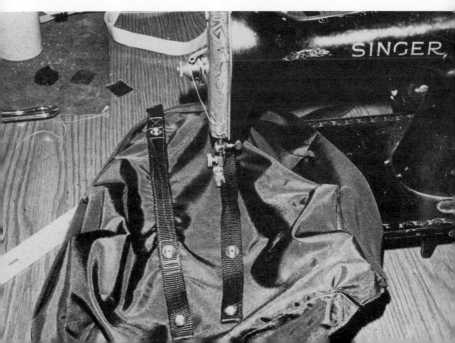

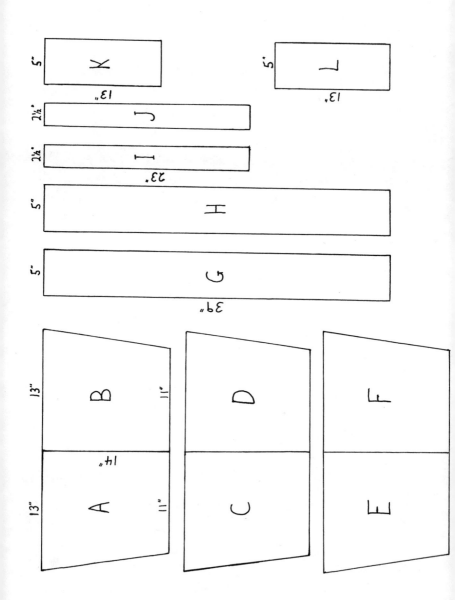

PANNIERS MATERIALS LIST

1 yard, 3 inches coated nylon fabric, medium or heavy, 44″ wide (if handlebar pack is also made, 2 yards are more than enough for everything)

22″ by 13″ sheet of aluminum or steel, thick enough for moderate stiffness (doubled sheeting from large tin cans can be used)

3 yards flat nylon webbing, ½″ or wider

6 small snap hooks to be sewn on webbing, large enough to go over carrier

1 buckle for webbing

2—22″ zippers, single or double slider

(optional—rivets and tool for setting them)

INSTRUCTIONS—PATTERN—PANNIERS

Lay out the pattern and cut it. The orientation shown is set up to make the pattern easy to understand, but it should be laid out to minimize wasted fabric. Pieces A, C, and E are identical, and B, D, and F are mirror images.

Straps should be installed first on the uncoated sides of A and D. The drawing shows the proper method, but the exact positioning should be carefully determined by checking against your own carrier and bike. The top hooks go over the carrier rods, and the lower hook goes on whatever fixture is available at the bottom. The hooks should be positioned so that the pannier is held just where it is wanted. The slanted side goes forward, and it must be positioned so that the heel will clear it easily. The hooks should fit the carrier exactly. About 6″ free webbing should be left at the top of each of the middle straps for later installation of a buckle. The snap springs on the hooks shown in the illustration have been broken off, but they should be left on until the panniers are completed, in case fitting is not done perfectly.

Sew A and B together, coated sides facing in, on three sides to form an envelope. Do the same with C and D. Cut the stiffening sheet into two pieces the same shape as the envelopes; each piece will be 13″ high, 12″ long at the top, and 10″ long at the bottom. Tape the edges of the stiffeners carefully with adhesive or electrical tape. Insert the stiffeners into the envelopes and sew the edges closed. Riveting at three or four points along each of the webbing straps will improve the panniers, but it is not essential.

The stiffened pieces are the inner sides of the panniers, and E and F are the outer sides. G and H are sewn between, forming the front, bottom, and rear walls. Sew G around one stiffened piece. Sew E or F to the other long edge of G. Sew the other pannier the same way. Sew K to the top of the stiffened side of one pannier and L to the other, forming the top flaps.

Sew one side of a zipper to the top three sides opposite the flap on each pannier. I and J should be folded double along their length to form rain flaps for the zippers. Sew them and the top edges of the zippers to the top flaps of the panniers.

Check the fit of the panniers and install the tightening buckle on one strap.

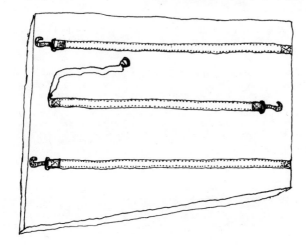

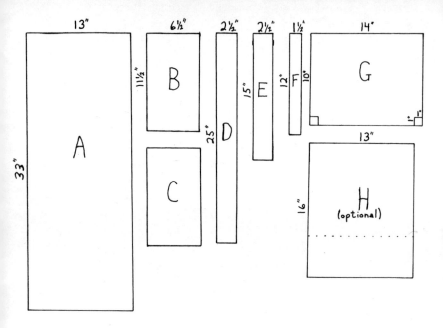

HANDLEBAR PACK MATERIALS LIST

1 yard coated nylon fabric, medium or heavy, 44" wide

2 yards flat nylon webbing, ½" or wider

1—24" zipper with two sliders

4" Velcro tape

Baby durable snaps and setting tool (available from Frostline) or equivalent

12" by 15" sheet of aluminum or steel (optional for stiffener)—can be cut from large tin can

INSTRUCTIONS—PATTERN—HANDLEBAR PACK

You should decide whether you want to include a stiffener in the pack, depending on what you want to carry in it and the type of rack you have. If raingear and similar bulky items are carried, a lighter pack without a stiffener will often do nicely; one can be added later with a bit more trouble. H is an extra panel to enclose the stiffener.

If the stiffening piece of metal is used, tape it all around the edges with adhesive or electrical tape, to prevent wear on the fabric. Take especial care at the corners, which may need to be rounded with tin snips or a file. Lay H to match one end of A, and sew around three sides. Insert the stiffener and sew the fourth side. Bend the stiffener so that A will bend at a right angle 11" down its length. This makes the stiffener into an L-shape, the long leg of which will be the back of the pack and the short leg the bottom.

Sew B and C into the sides of A. If the stiffener has been used, start by sewing one of the long sides of B to one of the long sides of the L-shape, then continue along the short side of B and the other long side. Sew C in the same way on the other side of A. The basic pack shape is now formed, with the loose flap formed by the end of A, which will be the cover.

One side of the zipper can now be sewn in along the upper edge of the pack. The other side of the zipper is sewn along the edge of the flap with D sewn over it doubled as a rain flap. G is the main piece for the front pocket. The 1" squares shown should be cut out, and the inside edges left should be sewn together, forming the pocket 12" wide, 9" high, and 1" thick, which can then be sewn to the front of the pack (opposite the stiffened back and the zipper opening). One side of the Velcro tape should be sewn ½" below the top edge. F is the top to this pocket and E the rain flap. One side of E is sewn around three sides of F, E is hemmed, the remaining Velcro sewn to E, and the whole flap sewn to the pack over the top of the pocket.

The pack is now complete except for fastening straps. The webbing straps are sewn on the pack all the way around for support, with the ends used to wrap around the carrier for snap attachment. The positioning of the straps will depend on the carrier used on the bike, so the exact attachment cannot be shown here. One of the advantages of making your own pack is that you can custom-fit the straps. One arrangement of straps and snaps is shown in a photo. Be sure to use enough snaps to prevent the bag from being shaken loose.

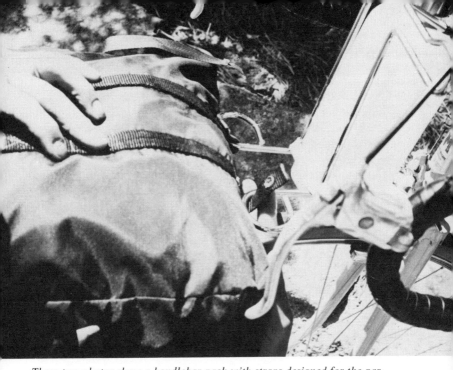

These two photos show a handlebar pack with straps designed for the particular carrier used. Heavy snaps attach the bag at the bottom and top. Two additional straps go around the brake handles to stabilize the pack. Anyone making a bag should fit a strap arrangement for the carrier he has.

ing forward, lightweight shields can be made of plastic, net, or nylon and be stretched between the seat and chain stays.

One solution to the carrier problem is to make one. The author has found that a good method is to get a molded plastic child's chair, remove the legs, and attach the seat directly to a sturdy rear carrier with U-bolts. Holes and a seat belt are easily added to this seat, and there is no problem putting rear panniers on. Spoke guards of one of the types mentioned have to be added. It may be necessary to block the seat up slightly in front to make it comfortable, but this will depend on the particular design.

For really young children a handlebar carrier may be satisfactory, but older children add too much weight for this to be suitable. Infants too young to sit will normally be carried in some sort of a backpack that will give them head support and keep them close to parent.

Trailers

Very light trailers are made for towing behind bicycles. Though it is possible to conceive of circumstances in which they might be necessary, the cyclist contemplating using one should consider eliminating some equipment first. Perhaps a group with one excessively strong and enthusiastic member might want to get a trailer for him to tow, adding rocks on the hills when this seemed necessary, but a less expensive alternative might be to have him ride a one-speed bicycle.

If, by any chance, one should find himself towing a trailer, downhill stretches should be taken slowly, regardless of the efficiency of the bicycle's brakes. The trailer will ruin the normal downhill handling characteristics and is particularly likely to throw the rear wheel into a skid if any braking is done on a sharp curve.

7

The Art of Riding

Those cyclists who come to bicycle camping from an extensive background of touring or racing will need little advice on riding, though they will have to adjust to riding with heavier loads and against more wind resistance. They will also have to learn a good deal of extra caution on downhill runs, because the packs make a bicycle considerably less stable at the same time they are reducing braking efficiency and increasing momentum.

Beginning cyclists and many commuters, on the other hand, often have very inefficient cycling styles, and they will really benefit from a little self-imposed training, in order to get a maximum amount of forward motion for the energy expended in pedalling. In riding as children and then as unconditioned adults, most of us picked up a lot of bad habits, and it is well worth while to rid oneself of at least a few of them to get maximum enjoyment from bicycle camping.

Pace, Rhythm, and Cadence

Most novice cyclists tend to pedal too slowly, often in too high a gear. Without going into technical and controversial dissertations on ideal cadences, it is safe to say that most tourists get maximum efficiency by pedalling at around 70-80 turns of the crank per minute. As an experiment, you can take your bike out, after you are used to it, and work into a comfortable pace on a level stretch of road. You can check the number of complete turns your feet are making each minute against a watch. If the rate is much below 70 rpm, you should experiment with faster pedalling for a while, to see if it improves your riding.

To develop a good pedalling speed, try taking a couple of long rides over fairly easy terrain. Keep the bicycle in a fairly low gear for the whole ride, so that pedalling is quite easy. Try pedalling at 75 rpm for a while, maintaining a steady rate. Remember to keep gear ratios low—the idea at this stage is to find your natural rhythm. After working on this for a while, you should have a pretty good feel for the pedalling rate which works well for you.

The most important trick for efficient riding is to maintain this rhythm, or cadence, fairly steadily as one rides along. Get out of the habit of start-stop pedalling—pushing along for a couple of minutes and then stopping altogether. Try to keep the feet going at roughly the same rate uphill and down, shifting gears down when the pedalling gets too hard, and shifting up when the legs can't keep up enough to give any push to the bike. After some practice, you will probably find yourself riding much more efficiently.

These recommendations on maintaining tempo are, of course, intended as flexible rules. When hills become steep enough, the pace slows even in the lowest gear, and cadence is not checked constantly with a stop watch once learned. It is worth noting, however, that the better the rider, the more he tends to keep up a steady tempo, mile after mile, uphill and down. This is the way the muscles work most efficiently.

The pace of the day is as important to the touring cyclist as his cadence. If the pace is set too slow, one tends to feel sluggish and tired, as if the muscles are bored. The most common mistake for beginners, though, is to start too fast in the morning and burn out before noon. Experienced riders have an easier time of it, because they can suit their pace easily to the amount of ground they want to cover that day. Novices should remember that the ride will not be much fun if the weaker members of the party are exhausted from eleven o'clock on.

It is usually best to start at quite a slow pace, allowing the muscles to warm up gradually. Pedal at a normal speed, but keep the gear ratios low so the muscles don't have to strain. If the day's journey begins with a vicious hill, a cold morning and creaky muscles may even make a walking start advisable, especially if some members of the group are out of condition.

Stopping schedules are largely a matter of personal or group choice, but long stops necessitated by exhausted muscles indicate too hard a pace. Such stops eat up a lot of time, and it is hard to get moving again. Slowing the pace and making shorter stops will speed overall progress and make it more comfortable. Sightseeing stops are a different matter altogether, and require balancing only against whatever progress the tourist has in mind to make that day.

On long trips, there is also some need to keep an eye on the overall pace of the journey. Trying to make too many miles the first day may well put the muscles off for the next forty-eight hours, especially since most people heading off on long tours are just starting vacations and are not in shape for long-distance cycling. Just as it is best to warm up slowly early in the day, trip progress is usually best if the first day or two are kept to a fairly easy pace. This gives the body time to adjust to the new regimen, and by the third day, everyone is really going well.

Position and Pedalling

Cyclists who haven't done a lot of riding over long distances should experiment with riding positions. The fully dropped position with the hands low on the bars is the most efficient one for delivering the maximum amount of power to the rear wheel, while at the same time decreasing wind resistance to a minimum. It is the standard racing position, and it is well worth practicing so that it can be used well for considerable periods. As a rule, however, touring cyclists move around a lot, changing from one position to another, and particularly favoring one sitting halfway up with the hands near the center of the bars. Changing positions frequently shifts the body's weight to different muscles and different parts of the hands, helping to prevent undue fatigue.

It is a good idea to get used to riding with the weight on the fleshy areas of the hands, shifting occasionally from one to another. The most natural position, in which much of the weight rests in the center of the heel of the hand, often causes numb hands after a few hours of riding. This is caused by pressure on one of the main nerves running across the palm. Using the fleshy parts of the hands to bear one's weight and switching hand positions are the best preventives, but bicycle gloves (which have some padding across the palms) help, and some people even tape padding onto their handlebars.

It is important to develop a pedalling motion which follows the circle of the cranks. The beginner usually just pushes down on each stroke, but pedalling becomes far more efficient when pushing forward at the top of the stroke and back at the bottom. With cleats and rattrap pedals one can also pull up at the back stroke. The trick is to *pedal in circles, not just up and down.* Ankling, which is much discussed, is simply the angling of the foot to use the circular motion more efficiently. Ankling is worth practicing, since it makes one's pedalling more powerful, but even racers don't ankle all the time.

The front part of the foot goes up with the upward pedal stroke and down with the downward part. This motion decreases the distance the legs have to travel with each stroke of the pedals. More importantly, it uses the muscles in the lower half of the leg to add extra power to each turn of the crank. For practice, the beginner should try ankling for several miles at a time, pushing the pedal down and back with the ball of his foot at the front bottom of the stroke and pulling the basket up with the top of his toes at the back of the stroke.

Bicycling gloves. These have ventilated backs and padded palms.

Hills

Hills are both the bane and joy of the cyclist's existence. He sweats up them, curses them, but often loves them. They are the spice of the day's ride, and sometimes the gristle as well. Any real tricks to riding up them are merely the practical application of proper pacing and gear changing. In carrying camping gear on a long day's trip, it is particularly important to conserve energy on the hills. Pedalling madly on the approach is tiring and ineffective. The regular cadence should be maintained on approaching the hill, and gears should be shifted down early—shifting late is hard on the derailleur and the cyclist. It is important not to burn out on the hills; speed going up should take second place to staying within one's physical limits. Of course, maintaining cadence is good if it is not too taxing, and there is nothing wrong with working up a good sweat—physical effort is part of the purpose of the trip. Still, the beginner should beware of working too hard to keep up, since he will lose far more time dragging himself along for the rest of the day than he can possibly make up on a few hills. The pace should be slowed first, and if the hill is still too hard, it may be best to get off and walk up.

Hills look a lot better on the downhill side, but some prudence is required, particularly by those carrying heavy loads on their bikes for the first time. Thirty extra pounds strapped on the bike make it handle very differently, particularly at high speeds and in emergency maneuvers. Braking is much less effective, and on steep hills, it is often necessary to brake frequently at relatively slow speeds to avoid getting out of control. Beware of traffic problems, loose gravel, turns, chuckholes, and bumps, any of which can easily dump a loaded bike travelling at high speed. The best rule is simply to ride conservatively until lots of practice in handling a loaded bike has been acquired.

Surviving the Traffic

By far the greatest danger faced by the bicycle camper is that he must usually share the road with far larger and faster vehicles. The practice of defensive driving is a necessity for any cyclist who wants to survive. Questions of fault and right-of-way are of secondary importance to the bicycle rider dealing with traffic, for if push comes to shove he is a guaranteed loser.

The first thing any cyclist must learn about the driver of an automobile is that there is a good chance of his being blind. Drivers of cars have trained themselves to see other large motor vehicles and to react to them, but many motorists simply do not notice smaller, slower moving objects. There is always a very good chance that a driver will literally not see a bicycle—the image just never registers in his brain! In some areas, most motorists are accustomed to cyclists, but even in these places the bike rider always has to be on the watch for the driver who is not. It is generally safest to assume that all cars are driven by children of low intelligence who are too small to see over the dashboards.

Naturally, the safest course to follow under the circumstances is to avoid the cars altogether. This is rarely feasible, but by a judicious choice of route and travelling time, it is often possible to stay away from most traffic. Secondary roads which parallel freeways are often free of traffic and are usually the most pleasant routes of travel.

Avoidance of traffic will also frequently drive the cyclist off the main travelled part of the road onto the edge, shoulder, and perhaps even the ditch. It is a perpetual source of annoyance that one must frequently ride in litter, debris, and broken beer bottles to avoid being run down, but it is a fact of life. The cyclist has a perfect right to the main part of the road, of course, but it will do him no good if he is run over asserting it.

Most motorists are not deliberately hostile to the cyclist, and they will pass giving a wide margin, providing they see him. Hence, one of the better ways to insure a pleasant trip is to increase one's own visibility. Bright colored clothing is a big help. International orange or day-glow pink vests or patches on the backs of shirts and shorts are a big help, especially on dull days. Some cyclists use flags on lightweight wands sticking up from the cycle, and this method has proven extremely effective, though the flapping banner may prove to be too annoying to many.

Given the good will of most motorists and the vulnerability of all cyclists, it is downright stupid to obstruct the road deliberately and to annoy automobile drivers unnecessarily. Riding several bicycles abreast and refusing to yield the right-of-way will certainly get the operator of a car angry at the time, and it may also leave him wanting to get back at cyclists in the future. Ride bicycles side-by-side only when traffic is very light, and stay prepared to move into single file whenever it is necessary to allow a car to pass easily. Two cyclists riding abreast should agree in advance who will drop back and who will pull forward.

Keeping as far right as possible on the travelled part of the pavement is standard riding procedure when riding with traffic on the road. All cyclists should practice riding in a straight line without weaving. Both safety and efficient cycling require that the rider avoid swinging back and forth over several feet of road. Practice riding on white border lines. A skilled cyclist should be able to stay right on the line. If rough pavement or some other obstruction is going to force him to pull out further onto the pavement, the cyclist must always check to be sure he is not going to steer into the path of an approaching car or truck.

Trucks can be a greater hazard to cyclists than cars, especially on older narrow highways which still are used as shipping routes. Besides taking a wide space on the road, truckers are more reluctant to slow down than autos, and they tend to be more confident of their judgment. In consequence, truckers are often willing to sail past a cyclist at sixty miles per hour, leaving only a foot of clearance. Aside from the danger of being hit, the cyclist experiences a heavy wind blast in such an encounter, and it may sometimes be hard to keep the bicycle steady. Unnerving encounters like this are sufficient to persuade most bicycle campers to avoid routes with heavy truck traffic like the plague. Some of the old U.S. highways are the worst spots in this respect. On long trips, it may be well to inquire of local cycling clubs or highway patrols to try to avoid being trapped on truck routes. Secondary roads can often be taken to get away from the behemoths. Truck traffic is harder to avoid by changing travelling time than cars are, since truckers generally drive at odd hours too. Early morning hours are usually best though, and even avoiding cars helps a little, since the trucks will more often be able to pull out into the road away from a bike when there is no approaching traffic. Advance planning is the best solution, however. Without it one may sometimes even be forced into choosing a super-highway, which at least has wide shoulders, rather than a narrow route heavily used by trucks going at high speeds.

As a general rule, however, superhighways should be avoided and, in fact, it is often illegal for cyclists to use them. Though there are wide shoulders, these are usually littered with debris and are subject to bombardment by cars which are out of control, making emergency stops, and the like. On occasion, one may be forced to travel a stretch of such a highway if it is the only connecting link available. Applicable laws should be checked. In many states, such sections must be open to all traffic (including bicycles) when no alternative routes are avilable. When forced to travel on superhighways, bicyclists must use extreme care, remembering that on these roads especially, motorists are not expecting to encounter them. In constricted spots and those with limited visibility, such as ramps, bridges, and underpasses, the cyclist will often have to stop and wait for a clearing in traffic or walk along outside the guard rails in order to maintain even a semblance of safety.

On all roads cyclists should be particularly aware of one frequent hazard involving motor vehicles. Car drivers generally think of bicycles as essentially stationary, when they see them at all. The operator of an automobile is often quite unaware that the bicycle he is passing may be travelling at twenty miles per hour. Thus, drivers making right turns will often pass a cycle and cut immediately into a right turn, pushing the bicyclist off the road and often running him down. This is probably the most common accident affecting experienced and safe riders, because it is so much harder to avoid than other hazards from cars. Since the auto in this type of accident comes from behind and is already endangering the cyclist when it comes into view, it is hard to take evasive action until it is too late. The only way to avoid this danger is to get in the habit of checking for it whenever one is approaching side roads and turn-offs.

Most of the other really common traffic hazards are less frequently encountered by the camping cyclist, who spends most of his time out in the country. They must still be watched while going through towns along the way, however. Parked cars must always be viewed with a jaundiced eye by the passing cyclist, who should get in the habit of watching for people inside who may suddenly open doors in front of him or pull out into his path. Storm grates, trolley or railroad tracks, and expansion joints in bridges frequently present traps for bicycle wheels and slippery spots in wet weather. Local traffic regulations may present another kind of hazard, and they should be obeyed scrupulously.

The Special Problems of Riding With a Load

Anyone who has never ridden with a load should take a bit of extra care when he first gets out on the road with a full complement of camping gear. The handling characteristics of a bike are bound to be different even if they are quite good, once twenty to thirty pounds of camping equipment are strapped on. Different loadings will produce different characteristics, too. It is a good idea to do a little maneuvering at various speeds at the beginning of the day to make sure everything is fastened securely and to check the handling of the bike. Then if there is a need to swerve when going at a good clip later in the day, the rider will have a better idea of what his bike is going to do.

Steering is particularly affected by loading on the front wheel. One can hardly expect the bike to be as responsive with fifteen pounds loaded into front panniers. Obviously, this is a good reason to keep loads as light as possible, so that one need not put much weight in front packs. When such loading cannot be avoided, however, it really isn't hard to ride the bike safely. It is simply necessary to recognize that handling is somewhat more sluggish and to ride accordingly

As has been mentioned previously, reduced braking efficiency should be expected when one is riding with a load, so that special care may be needed on steep grades to avoid losing control. Some care must be exercised to avoid skids when one is braking, particularly on corners. A loaded bike is usually much more prone to skidding.

The behavior of the bike at speed should be carefully noted. Some bikes have a tendency to vibration and swerving in the front when they are loaded, particularly bikes with pronounced fork rakes. If this tendency is noticed, the cyclist should take extra care in risking high speed downhill runs, since hitting even a pebble or sand patch may throw him completely out of control.

Bicycle campers have to anticipate extra wind resistance because of their loads. A front bag and rear panniers, which generally make up the minimum set of packs carried by the cycle camper, create a tremendous amount of extra aerodynamic resistance, and fighting against a headwind can be really exhausting with a load. Dropping into the lowest possible riding position will help a little, but frequently tourists will have to revise their schedules or routes, planning to stop at a closer campsite or calling a rest for a few hours until the wind changes.

Working with Mother Nature

The more he gets out in the elements, the more the cyclist is likely to find it to his advantage to work with rather than against them. Wind is one of the cases in point. It is nice occasionally to ride right into the teeth of a good wind, but the touring cyclist is likely to find that he gets plenty of opportunity for this without making any effort to seek it out. Sometimes there is no way to avoid beating against the wind, but frequently a little study and thought will enable the camping bicyclist to take advantage of normal patterns.

Many areas have daily wind patterns quite apart from weather systems which may move through, and the studious bicycle rider can take advantage of them. In mountainous areas during the warmer months there are frequently upslope breezes which develop by midmorning and blow through most of the afternoon, only to be replaced by downslope valley winds when the air begins to cool in the late afternoon or evening. Along the shores of the ocean and large lakes the differential warming of the land will generally produce onshore winds in the heat of the day and offshore ones as things cool off. Careful planning will enable the cyclist to take advantage of these daily patterns instead of fighting them in both directions.

Most regions also have prevailing winds which vary with the season. Picking the right time of year for some trips will make them more pleasant. These prevailing winds often have daily patterns, also, which should be checked in advance, or at least observed with an intelligent eye. After three days of beating against the wind that always comes up at two in the afternoon, a crafty rider will start earlier in the morning and be at camp by that time the next day. Though there are regional and seasonal variations, the wind generally tends to come up in the afternoon and be quietest around dawn. So if you are having wind problems on a trip, "early to bed and early to rise" may be the solution to getting there—whether it makes you healthy, wealthy, and wise, or not.

For trips around his own area, the cyclist will find that careful watching of the weather maps on the tube will give him a fund of information to use in planning trips. Getting a general idea of wind patterns, the way that storms come in, and similar tidbits will help him to be going in the right direction at the right time. For planning rides farther afield, the *National Atlas of the United States* has wind maps of the country for each month of the year. One can also get information from local offices of the weather bureau about wind patterns in any given area.

Other little natural unpleasantries that beset the cyclist often follow daily patterns, too. Afternoon thunderstorms are common in many places on summer afternoons, and the wise cycle camper will usually be off the road and have his tent set up before they hit, unless the heat is so bad that being drenched is a welcome prospect.

It almost goes without saying that weekend trips are usually planned for good weather. Cyclists on longer journeys may have to grin and bear long periods of rain, but cycling is more pleasant as a fair weather sport. Cycling in cold weather can be a pleasant experience for many of us, but wheeling along in the rain is generally endured rather than enjoyed. It's a lot easier to enjoy backpacking in the rain than bicycling; at least when you're backpacking, the water wetting you is clean and coming from generally upwards. When cycling, you'll find it comes from just about everywhere: down from the sky, up, back, and forwards from your wheels, and sideways from passing trucks. And three-quarters of it is dirty. However, human beings are adaptable, and those who live in rainy areas end up alleging that they *like* to ride in the rain after a while.

8

Special Riding Conditions

There are a number of situations that the camping cyclist will run across from time to time, by accident or design, which call for particular skills or precautions. Though a properly loaded bike is reasonably stable in normal circumstances, special care sometimes has to be exercised. Other sorts of precautions have to be taken when riding in an environment that may present unusual problems or danger, as in the desert.

Riding in the Rain

Rain presents perhaps the most common situation of this kind. As has already been suggested, avoidance is perhaps the best wet weather solution, but sooner or later every bicycle camper is bound to be caught by a spell of wet weather, and if tours are planned in some areas wet weather riding will probably be unavoidable.

157

Fenders and mud flaps are almost a necessity if much riding in the rain is anticipated. They will not eliminate road spray, but the drenching will at least be kept to manageable levels. If precipitation and traffic are light, fenders and mud flaps may be sufficient protection for the lower body. Sweating is much less of a problem when only a rain cape or parka has to be worn.

In warm weather it may be possible to ignore the lower part of the body even without fenders, though the legs are bound to get pretty dirty from splashes. A longish parka will protect the seat, however, and if shorts are worn wet clothing on the lower body is no problem. The main sources of discomfort in this situation are likely to be the feet. Even if rain booties are worn, they will not be completely effective if they are worn alone without rain pants. Reasonably heavy wool socks will not keep the feet dry, but they will make them more comfortable.

In heavy rain, unless the weather is very warm, a complete rain suit must normally be worn. The rain parka and pants shown in patterns in this book are an example of a good outfit. Booties can be made of coated nylon, like those in the patterns, or very lightweight overshoes can be carried, either the stretchy rubber or the plastic kind. If these are worn over bicycle shoes with cleats, holes can be cut in the bottoms to fit the cleats. The greatest difficulty with a full rain suit is that inevitably a great deal of perspiration condenses inside, leaving one sometimes feeling that the suit is wetter inside than out. The more ventilation that can be managed, the less of a problem this will be. Keeping physical effort within reasonable bounds will minimize perspiration and thus condensation.

If the weather is cold, rain presents a serious chilling problem. The rain itself cools the body and soaks clothing, and then evaporation of this moisture robs the cyclist of more heat. All these difficulties are increased by wind chill created by movement of the bicycle and rider through the air, even in the absence of external wind. If such weather is anticipated, wool clothing, which maintains a good deal of insulation when wet, should be carried. Some synthetic insulation also has this virtue. If the cyclist encounters cold wet weather when lots of extra clothing is not being carried, camp should be made early. Cold, wet weather is by far the most dangerous kind for outdoorsmen, since the body can be robbed of heat so rapidly that death by exposure is a danger. Even before this stage is reached, lowered body temperatures impair coordination and judgment.

Considerable care is required when riding in wet weather. Visibility is decreased and many normally good surfaces become very slippery. Wet leaves are almost as slick as glare ice. Perhaps an even greater hazard is created by the decreased visibility experienced by automobile drivers. In the best of conditions, many motorists will not notice a bicycle, and in rainy weather the problem is greatly exacerbated. Cyclists also tend to be less attentive, lowering their heads into the rain and paying far less attention to traffic. One must concentrate on avoiding this temptation, since the cyclist desiring a long touring career has to ride with extreme caution and attention in the rain.

Riding in the Mountains

Because of the steep and continuous grades involved, clearly the first prerequisite for mountain riding is that the cyclist be in reasonably good shape or have his bike equipped with a very low climbing gear. The stringency of these requirements will depend on the particular trip; the gradient and duration of the hills are as important as the actual elevation gain. It is far easier to climb 5,000 feet in 20 miles than in 10.

Cyclists riding in the mountains for the first time, particularly with camping gear, should exercise a good deal of caution on downgrades. It is not at all difficult to hit speeds of 40 miles per hour or so when descending mountain roads on a loaded bicycle, and braking down from high speeds can be time consuming. The cyclist should anticipate the possibility of loose sand and gravel on turns, of chuckholes, of motorists coming around curves on the wrong side of the road, and the thrills of the downhill plunge should be modified accordingly. All these cautions apply even more strongly if the rider is not familiar with the handling characteristics of his bicycle during emergency maneuvers with a load at high speeds.

Bicycle camping in the mountains often requires extra stamina and extra equipment. In Rocky Mountain National Park.

Braking should be applied to both wheels. Some braking must always come on the rear wheel to prevent the bicycle from flipping forward, but the major stopping power comes from the front brake, because if the bicycle is slowing rapidly most of the load goes onto the front wheel. Since this is the case, braking too hard on the rear wheel will cause it to skid, particularly on a curve or on loose gravel. If a patch of gravel is seen ahead, it is usually best to steer straight through it with the brakes completely off to prevent a skid from starting.

If dirt or gravel roads are taken through the mountains, strong tires should be used. The cyclist should try to watch for large or sharp stones and avoid them if possible. Tires should be cleared periodically with a gloved hand if tire savers are not used, in order to avoid punctures caused by sharp bits of rock working into the rubber. Descents on dirt and gravel roads should be very slow and cautious, since a turn while the bicycle is travelling at a good clip is almost certain to result in a fall.

Weather in the mountains is quite changeable, and bicycle campers should be well-prepared for all possibilities with extra clothing that will retain its warmth even in wet weather. Long pants, wool gloves or mittens, heavy wool socks, a warm shirt or sweater, a good hat, and a windproof jacket or parka should be considered as a minimum. The possible weather conditions for a particular range of mountains and time of year should be checked carefully in advance, since even more clothing often has to be carried to provide reasonable comfort and safety. The new initiate to mountain travel should be aware that a hot sun during the morning hours can frequently be followed by icy rain and snow the same day, often with rather brief warning.

Particular care should be taken with sun protection at high altitude, even on cloudy days. Less ultraviolet radiation is filtered out by the atmosphere at high elevations, and these are the rays which cause burns. Sunglasses and sun creams should be put on earlier than usual on trips over high passes in the Rockies or the Sierra Nevada.

Cold Weather, Ice, and Snow

Though long bicycle tours can be taken in cold weather, it is usually best to confine them to periods when clear roads can be expected. Riding in ice and snow is a slow and tricky business, particularly on a bicycle loaded with camping gear. Warm shoes which do not fit too tightly should be worn with heavy wool socks. Other clothing should be carried in a number of layers, so that clothing can be easily added and taken off. For example, one might start the morning wearing cycling shorts, long wool pants, wind pants, a net undershirt, a wool shirt, a sweater, a wind parka with a hood, and a wool hat. As exercise warms the body, various layers can be removed, and at rest stops they can be put back on. Clothing should always be taken off before heavy sweating makes it damp. Clearly, particular clothing choices will depend on how cold the weather really is, but it is better to carry too much clothing than to be caught without enough in a cold weather camping situation.

Though riding in cold weather on *dry* roads is really quite pleasant, actually travelling for more than short distances in snow and ice is usually the product of miscalculation rather than design. If the snow is wet and slushy, conditions are similar to those in rainy weather. Tires generally cut through to the wet road surface, and wet weather gear has to be worn or the rider will be soaked. Dry snow is not difficult, unless it gets deep. Packed snow does not affect riding too much, and the cyclist will usually find he has fair traction if ice patches can be avoided. Soft snow requires some effort for pedalling, but does not create a major problem until it becomes deep enough so that the feet dig in at the bottom of each stroke. Crusty snow or snow which has been soft and then frozen into ruts and blocks is a curse, and it is often as easy to walk the bike in such conditions.

Ice is the real hazard for the cold weather cyclist. On an ice patch, the bicycle rider is practically helpless—the slightest bump or attempt to maneuver will make a fall inevitable. Anticipation is critical for safe riding. Either the rider should dismount or ride straight across slowly and carefully, ready to put a foot down if the wheels slip. Ice patches should be particularly expected where snow melt has run across the road and cooled, at intersections where cars spin their wheels starting across, and on hills in the same circumstances.

Cleats with tight toe clip straps should never be worn in cold weather when there is a possibility of ice patches, since the combination will prevent getting the feet out quickly in case of a fall.

Clearly, the comments made earlier about the dangers of automobiles and trucks apply even more to cold weather riding, par-

ticularly in snow, than to any other time. The cyclist must anticipate fogged windshields, drivers' inattention, and their loss of
control on slippery spots.

Riding in the Desert

Many of the desert regions of North America present nearly
ideal touring conditions for the camping cyclist, providing
proper judgment is exercised in picking the season and tactics
for the ride. There are good roads with only moderate traffic in
a number of deserts, together with spectacular scenery, reasonable gradients, guaranteed good weather, and unlimited possibilities for camping. In spring, the combination of beautiful flow-
ers and pleasant temperatures is particularly attractive.

The special problems of riding in the desert are pretty obvious. Water may not be available for long stretches, and so it has
to be carried. Adequate quantities are essential. Cycling in hot,
dry weather can suck tremendous amounts of moisture from the
body. Furthermore, enough water has to be carried for any con-
tingencies, such as the extra time required to fix a few flats. If a
completely dry day must be planned, a gallon of water per
person per day should be the minimum carried. Containers must
be reliable and should be carried so that they cannot be punctured. It is also best to keep water in more than one container,
so that in case of accident there will always be some remaining.

If one is sweating heavily, it is best to take some salt tablets
along with drinking water. The number which may be required
varies with the rate of sweating, previous adaptation by the body
to heavy perspiration, and the amount of salt taken with food.
Four tablets per quart of water drunk would not be unreasonable
for someone not used to a great deal of heavy sweating. Muscle
cramps, indicate a salt deficit and the need for more tablets, with
plenty of water.

Sunburn should be avoided in the desert, as elsewhere, by
judicious use of creams and clothing. On hot days a hat should
be worn to protect the head and to help prevent heat exhaustion.
Some sort of light-colored cap with good ventilation is best. If

the heat is felt too much, the cyclist should stop until he cools down, and then proceed to ride at a slower pace. A tarp or poncho makes a good shelter because it can be quickly pitched with the bicycle to provide shade if needed.

The best way to avoid real heat problems is to travel in the cooler seasons. Winter travel is good in some places, while spring and fall weather are the most pleasant in those farther north or at higher altitude. April would be a good month in Utah, for example. If one does get stuck with weather too hot for reasonable riding in midday, travel can be restricted to the very early morning and late evening hours to avoid the worst heat. In really difficult situations and emergencies when water is in short supply, riding can be done at night, with activity during the day kept to a minimum.

One other problem in many desert areas is that of thorns. There are several types of vines and cacti frequently found, particularly in the Southwest, which are notorious in their abilities to puncture tires. Vigilance by the rider will avoid some of these problems. If he watches for the plants he will sometimes be able to avoid them. Even if he rides over them, stopping to inspect tires will usually allow the thorns to be removed before they cause problems, since it usually takes some time before they work through. Users of sew-ups should choose the toughest tires they can for desert rides, but problems should still be expected. Cyclists using clinchers may wish to use thorn-proof inner tubes for rides in the worst regions. Such tubes are very thick on surface towards the road and are rarely punctured, but they are also very heavy and should only be used where they are really needed.

Dirt and Gravel Roads

Protecting tires and rims requires some care when riding on primitive roads. Good riding technique is one of the major factors in avoiding trouble with this sort of travel. A cyclist who pays careful attention to the road surface, riding conservatively and avoiding objects which might damage his tires, shifting his weight when necessary to distribute weight equally between the two wheels, and walking on terrain that is so rough it might damage the rims, can often travel frequently on bad roads without experiencing much difficulty. On the other hand, a rider who expects his machine to take all the punishment of bad roads without his assistance is likely to run into frequent problems.

The need for care while riding downhill on dirt or gravel has already been mentioned. The possibility of skids also makes wearing cleats with tight pedal straps inadvisable. Ruts, hills, and bumps should be ridden across straight on, when possible, to prevent slips. If they are so steep that rims might be dented, the rider should stop and walk the bike over. Tire pressure should be checked before riding on rough roads. Underinflated tires will make skids a little less likely, but they will make tire damage probable and will almost guarantee damage to the rims and perhaps the spokes as well.

Riding at Night

Every caution concerning the invisibility of cyclists to motorists applies far more at night, of course, and most cyclists prefer to avoid night riding whenever possible. Regardless of precautions he may have taken, the cyclist riding at night must be perpetually alert to the possible necessity of running into a ditch to avoid a hurtling automobile. Finally, in this negative vein, the best portable light is still woefully inadequate for showing up road hazards, so even a careful rider will abuse his tires more in night riding than he ever would in the day.

With all this said, it is possible for anyone who anticipates some riding after dark to take advantage of the situation and greatly improve his safety. Automobiles use headlights at night, so if adequate reflective materials are used, the cyclist can often attract the attention of the motorist in the dark more easily than he can in the daytime. The little French lights which can be strapped to the leg have already been mentioned as excellent, and the reader may recall that the reason they are effective is that the up and down motion attracts the driver's eye far out of proportion to the size of the light. Two other principles may be mentioned here. Though drivers on the open road will be going faster and will be less likely to expect a cyclist than those in town, the bicycle rider is often safer in the country than in the city if he uses enough warning devices. This is because the multitude of bright lights in the city may confuse the motorist's eye, while on a country road there are fewer distractions. The second principle is that no light a cyclist can carry is nearly so effective for most purposes in warning motorists as reflectors are. Except for the leg light (some prefer one on each leg) and a lamp for his own vision of the road, the cyclist is best advised to concentrate on reflective materials.

The reflective tape made by 3M is particularly useful in making the cycle visible to motorists. Strips can be put on the backs of pedals, the heels of shoes, seat posts, the rear sides of packs, and so forth. Such strips and other reflectors should be carefully cleaned before any night riding, and should be rewiped periodically if necessary. Finally, if riding at night is planned, special clothing should be carried. A number of very lightweight but effective safety garments are available commercially or can be made at home. Vests, patches which face to the rear for shorts, panniers, or stuff sacks, and anklets with reflective patches are all useful. If enough of these devices are used, the cyclist will generally be able to ride at night with reasonable confidence of safety. In emergencies, light-colored clothing is much more visible than dark.

For a front lamp on the bicycle, a headlamp has already been mentioned as probably the most useful type. It is controlled by the movement of the rider's head, so it can be swung to concentrate on an obstacle or road detail ahead far more effectively than any light attached to the bicycle. It is also useful in situations where reflective devices are especially ineffective in warning vehicles of the bicycle's presence. The most common of these situations occurs when a motorist is entering a main road from a driveway or side street. He will look for bright car headlights and will probably not notice a weak bicycle light, particularly if it is not pointed directly at him. The cyclist should generally assume that the driver will not see him and should stop and wait for the car, but in cases where this isn't possible, shining the headlamp in the direction of the motorist and waggling it will usually attract the driver's attention.

When riding at night, the cyclist should try to avoid looking at the headlights of opposing traffic, since this will blind him for several seconds. It is all too easy to hit a chuckhole in the moments just after an oncoming car has passed, before the eyes become reaccustomed to the weaker light of the bicycle headlamp. Finally, it should go without saying that fast riding at night is usually very hazardous, except when the road is well known—rarely the situation for the bicycle camper. If speed is wanted it is usually best to bed down and get an early start, rather than trying to make good time after dark.

A French arm light. The best light to warn motorists of the night-riding cyclist, but it should be worn on the leg or the ankle.

9

Planning Bicycle Camping Tours

There are about as many ways to organize bike camping trips as there are cyclists who engage in them. The most common tour in Europe and among many North American cyclists, is one that proceeds from one hostel or other accommodation to another. Even cycle campers can use this method to advantage sometimes, stopping at commercial accommodations, hostels, or the houses of friends occasionally. Such a change of pace provides a refreshing chance for a shower and is often necessary if stops are to be made in cities. In the main, however, the bicycle camper will spend his nights out-of-doors, sometimes in organized campgrounds and sometimes just in a convenient patch of woods. One of the main aspects of planning a tour is checking on campsites for each expected night's stay.

With a rough idea of where he wants to go, the cyclist can get together some maps and perhaps some lists of campgrounds to try to figure the itinerary of the trip. In some areas, where camping spots are plentiful and there is no worry about overcrowding, this may be left to pot luck, but usually it cannot be. It is often vital to have a definite place in mind for the end of the day, and to know that a campsite will be available when one arrives. This planning of campsites really encompasses every aspect of the trip: the route, the distance that can be covered each day, the location of stores and water supplies, and so forth.

Before planning a route, one must consider the style of the trip. A few experienced bicycle campers can rely on chance if they wish, heading where the urge takes them at the speed they happen to enjoy at the moment. If night catches them, they will usually be able to find somewhere to bed down. With large groups much more careful planning is required, particularly if there are many beginners along. Campgrounds may be too full to handle the party, local landowners are not likely to agree to putting up a horde, and one is hardly likely to be able to bed thirty people down quietly in some local park. With large groups, every detail should be arranged in advance. Reservations need to be made if there is any possibility of running into full campgrounds. Arrangements have to be made with farmers for camping, and careful thought should be given to handling breakdowns, emergencies, and the like. Bus routes and schedules should be obtained, bicycle shops located, and so on, so that if one person needs to drop out, the matter can be handled smoothly.

A First Look

If a trip is going to be right around home, there will be little difficulty in making plans. The terrain will be well-known, any necessary arrangements can be made by phone, and if anyone's bike comes unglued or some other contingency arises, the resulting problems can be readily solved. Usually, though, preliminary planning has to be done with maps, guides, and letters. The point of departure should normally be a *good* detailed road map. Poor maps or large scale ones are generally useless to cyclist, because they mainly show only the roads he wants to stay far away from. The high-speed throughways should be avoided like the plague by the bicycle tourist, and even the secondary roads shown on maps covering large areas are usually not the best cycling routes, since they are normally the fastest roads between points. The cyclist should get the most detailed maps he can obtain. In National Forests and National Parks, writing the appropriate Park or Forest Supervisor will usually bring all the maps and information that are needed. For other areas, county road maps are usually of the scale needed by the cyclist. The best sources are state, city, and county Chambers of Commerce, state and county highway departments, and state park and wildlife departments. Auto clubs sometimes publish excellent regional maps, but this varies widely not only with the club but with the area. AAA, for example, puts out some excellent California regional maps, but little of comparable nature useful in Colorado.

Once he has obtained some reasonable maps, the camper can start to work out a route. The first question is clearly that of how far one can expect to travel each day. Experience on day trips is a necessary guide, and the planner obviously has to have a pretty good idea of the capacities of all those involved. Beginners should estimate very conservatively. Clearly, the least robust member of a party has to be the one considered most carefully. No one will enjoy a trip if it is much too ambitious for any participant.

Daily mileage depends on an interaction between the terrain, the weather, the cyclist, and his gear, a relationship which operates throughout the trip, not just on each single day. Hauling the weight and working against the wind-resistance of camping gear is quite different from cycling with just a spare sew-up and a bag lunch. One also does not usually feel like going "all-out" for day after day, so expectations should be scaled down accordingly, at least until there has been a few days' travel to get the cyclists toughened and tuned.

In general, a good daily figure for mileage would be about half what the least able member of the party could cover on a one-day trip from home and still find challenging but not totally exhausting. If one hundred miles can be covered in a single day, fifty miles is reasonable figure with gear on a long trip. This assumes roughly similar conditions. If a camping trip is in mountainous country and trial runs are only moderately hilly, distances should be halved again. The same rule applies to expected bad weather, headwind and to dirt or gravel road considerations. Twelve miles on a dirt road will probably be equivalent to twenty-five on pavement. Thus, if a hundred miles make a good day on a rolling Sunday ride near home, fifty would be reasonable on a camping trip in similar conditions, twenty-five would be more realistic pedalling through the Rockies, and if some of the gravel roads in those mountains were being traversed, even twelve or thirteen miles might not be a bad day's ride. Rain or headwinds might cut distance down still more. With experience, one can get a more accurate idea of one's own capacities and those of his companions, but these rules of thumb should help. They are good ones to follow for a while.

There are a few other special problems that should also be considered. Weather is important, and so is the group's attitude about it. Are the participants willing to ride in the rain? Just during afternoon thundershowers, or through all-day, steady rain? How much bad weather is there? Allowances should be made for bad-weather days, particularly if the trip is planned in a way that requires covering a certain distance. More rain has to be expected in the Maritime Provinces than the Sierra Nevada in summer, so that even if one is planning on doing some cycling in the rain, more stopover days would have to be planned in the former area than the latter.

Acclimatization may have to be considered if a vacation is being planned in a region that will exert unfamiliar strains on the body. High altitude requires some time before the body can be expected to function at all efficiently. Thus, if a trip was planned using motorized transportation from sea level to Reno, Nevada, and then setting out immediately up into the Sierra Nevada mountains, the first day should be very short and easy, and the second should still be on the conservative side, in order to allow the party to get used to exercise at altitude. Individuals vary greatly in the ease with which they acclimatize, and strength and physical condition have relatively little to do with it. Similar practices of working easily at first should be followed if one is taking a trip in an area much hotter than one is used to, in the desert for example.

Such preliminary planning might go this way. Suppose a trip were being planned by a small group from the East Coast in reasonable physical condition, planning on a two-week cycling vacation in the Colorado Rockies, with many climbs of difficult passes. They might start by assuming they would fly to Denver, spending the evening at a hotel or a friend's home and starting the next morning. To establish an overall trip plan, they allow two rest days, leaving twelve days for their trip. Though the weather in this area in the summer is fairly pleasant, they allow two bad-weather days. This leaves ten travelling days. The first day will be mostly in the plains, but it will also be a day for acclimatizing, so they figure on covering 25 miles. The rest of the first week will be in tough mountains, sometimes on dirt roads and with occasional afternoon thunderstorms, so 25 miles per day seems enough. This means 125 miles can be covered in the first week. For the second week, the group should be in better shape, and the members allow 35 miles per day for four days. On their final day, they will be coming back to Denver, so they should have mostly downhill going and figure on covering 50 miles. Thus, in the 14 days, they plan to cover 315 miles. Having this preliminary figure, they can pick a route that looks nice and begin working on detailed day-to-day plans. They can easily change things around later, because the plan is flexible. If it turns out they are going well ahead of schedule, they can take interesting side trips or hikes, or they can lengthen the circuit. If they are going slowly, they may be able to ride on a spare day or two, or they can shorten the circuit.

Daily Itinerary

Once the basic trip has been planned, one can go over maps and campground guides and make up a detailed daily itinerary, locating likely campgrounds, checking elevation gains, and allowing for possible headwinds and the like. It may be possible to find out enough about terrain from road maps and general knowledge of an area. In Kansas, for example, headwinds might turn out to be a problem, but long uphill climbs clearly would not. On the other hand, if one is planning to cross a major mountain range, one would expect severe and continuous grades, even if all details were lacking.

If extra information is wanted there are several possible sources. For terrain, the topographical maps issued by the U.S. Geological Survey will tell the cyclist all he needs to know about altitude gain and gradients. Most of the country is mapped in several series, of which the most useful to the cyclist is the 1:250,000 series, roughly one inch to four miles. These usually contain enough information to allow one to get exact mileage and elevation gain for any leg of the trip, while not requiring an absurd number of maps to cover the whole trip. The address of the Geological Survey office from which the maps can be obtained can be found in the appendix; index maps of each state showing the coverage of various maps and series, are available from the same offices free. The Survey maps must usually be supplemented by a recent road map, since they are often not up to date on highway construction.

Maps showing prevailing winds throughout the country during each month are published in the official *National Atlas of the United States,* which is available in most libraries. This same reference is useful for identifying temperature and rainfall patterns. Using this information, it is possible to get a pretty good idea of the conditions that will normally be encountered on any trip, even if one has never been in the area before.

Another excellent source of information is a local cyclist, particularly one who does a lot of touring in the region you want to visit. He will know when thunderstorms and local winds come up, what current road conditions are, whether tire-puncturing thorns should be expected, and is apt to have a host of other useful information. The distribution of this sort of information has been vastly simplified by the League of American Wheelmen. Besides engaging in other activities which benefit all cyclists, a roster of other members is sent to each person who joins, and almost any of them will be happy to assist others planning a tour in their area.

With all these sources, it is a fairly easy matter to plan a trip day by day, determining where one is going to stay each night, how many miles are going to be covered, and so on. Later on the cyclist may take quite a few trips without bothering to plan so thoroughly, but beginning tours are likely to be a lot happier if they are thought out carefully in advance.

Finding the Way

Bicycle campers usually have a pretty easy time finding their way around. They go more slowly than automobile drivers and are less likely to overlook obscure road signs, but, unlike back-packers they do have roads to guide them. Occasionally, one takes the wrong road, but this is rarely of serious consequence. Most cyclists do not carry compasses and many would not know how to use one properly.

There are some circumstances, however, in which special precautions are warranted. Trips to remote areas or along log-ging roads, for example, may require more knowledge of route-finding techniques. If trips like this are planned, it is important to carry accurate maps and compasses and to practice their use in advance. In particular, the beginner should note that compass direction almost always deviates from true direction by a certain amount. The degree and direction of this deviation for a partic-ular location has to be checked in advance, but it can range to as much as twenty-five degrees at some points within the contiguous United States. The deviation will be to the east of true north in the western part of the continent and to the west of true north in the eastern part of the continent.

It is very much to the cyclist's advantage to cultivate the art of reading contour maps. The usefulness of U.S.G.S. contour maps has been mentioned in connection with figuring elevation gains for any leg of the journey. This is the simplest use of the contour map; one simply counts the number of contour lines crossed in uphill portions of a trip and multiplies by the contour interval listed on the map. Such maps give an excellent representation of terrain, and the bicycle camper will get more out of his trips if he learns to visualize the landscape in advance of a trip by looking at maps. By carrying a contour map and associating the patterns with the surrounding terrain, the cyclist will learn to read them fairly painlessly. This knowledge will serve him in good stead on journeys along confusing networks of mining or logging roads.

Planning Equipment and Provisions

The necessary items for bicycle camping have already been mentioned elsewhere in this book, but the tourist has to decide at the beginning of each trip which of them he will need to carry. The information obtained from maps, guidebooks, climatic information, and correspondence finally has to be coordinated and conclusions formed. One has to decide how warm a sleeping bag is needed, what if any shelter has to be carried, what sort of clothing will be appropriate, how many water containers may have to be hauled, what food can be purchased on the road, whether to take a stove, and so on. Climatic information should be considered first. It will determine clothing, shelter, rain gear, bad weather days to be allowed, and it will influence the availability of water and fuel. Supply points have to be checked to see how often food can be purchased and how much water will have to be carried. These factors also will influence daily mileage, since travel will be slower if heavy loads have to be carried.

If towns are frequent, most food will be purchased along the way, and the only things that may need consideration in advance planning are for items like seasonings which can be packed more conveniently at home. Notes should be made of any long distances between supply points so that extra provisions can be purchased where necessary. If stores are likely to be closed on Sundays or holidays, this too should be considered.

Water is even more critical than food; it is a lot heavier and harder to do without. In most areas this is no real worry, since one can always stop at a farmhouse and ask permission to fill up water bottles. On long rides in arrid sections of the western states, however, farms can be few and far between. *The distance to water must be meticulously checked in advance in dry regions.* Riding a bicycle in hot, dry weather sucks the moisture out of the body so fast that it is hard to avoid becoming dehydrated even with enough water. Without it, one can reach a truly dangerous state very quickly. Assuming that one drinks as much as possible in the morning before breaking camp, at least two quarts per person should be allowed for drinking during the day, and this is likely to seem too little in really hot weather.

If water is not available in any of the campsites along the cycling route, extra containers will have to be carried for transporting water to camp. Collapsible plastic water bags can be used, or one can carry jugs or other containers. If only one section of a very long trip will require carrying large quantities of water, one can often pick up old bleach bottles at a laundromat. Properly cleaned, they make good water containers and they can be thrown in the trash when no longer needed.

A stove and fuel should be taken unless the supply of firewood is absolutely certain. In this day and age, there is no excuse for cutting live trees for fires, so if the camper misjudges, he will have to eat a cold meal or go to a restaurant. On trips of a week or less it is usually most convenient to carry all the necessary fuel, since it is hard to purchase along the way except in large quantities. I find that a full gasoline stove and a quart container of extra fuel is plenty for a week, but personal cooking habits will influence this somewhat. If camping in very cold weather is planned, more fuel must be carried.

Repair equipment that should be carried will be influenced by the remoteness of the trip, conditions of the roads to be travelled, and the duration of the trip. Long distances on back roads naturally dictate more complete emergency kits and preparations. One usually does not carry a wrench large enough to remove a freewheel, for example, though the freewheel tool itself should be carried. Unless special provisions are made, it is impossible to replace a broken spoke on the freewheel side of the rear wheel without removing the cluster, so a large wrench or a vise has to be borrowed at a gas station or elsewhere. On trips where the distance between gas stations is great, some special provision should be made. Large groups may want to carry one large wrench. Individuals can have their rear hubs drilled specially to allow replacement of spokes without removing the freewheel or can carry specially bent replacement spokes. (Both these methods are discussed in chapter 5.) Extra innertubes, tires, spokes, cables, and brake blocks are clearly dictated the farther one gets from bicycle shops.

Campgrounds: How to Choose and Find Them

There are many directories of campgrounds published these days, by motor clubs, oil companies, magazines, and others. These are useful to the bicycle camper for locating campgrounds and for checking facilities and fees that should be anticipated. Unfortunately, such directories are part of a trend which makes campgrounds less and less suitable for use by cyclists and other self-propelled campers. In a pinch, of course, the cyclist will put up with any sort of campsite, but the experience will be more pleasant if he picks and chooses, so a little care in this when planning the trip will be amply rewarded later on.

In general, campgrounds administered by public agencies are more suitable for cyclists and less expensive, though there are many exceptions. The bicycle camper should be particularly on the lookout for walk-in campgrounds, which are placed at some distance from the road. They may be anywhere from a hundred feet to a couple of miles from the parking lot, but they are always more pleasant than sites designed for motor vehicles. In most places, the more primitive campgrounds are likely to be more pleasant for the cyclist. Where possible, one should avoid facilities with "trailer hookups" (electricity, water, and sewer direct to the site), swimming pools, amusement parks, and so on. When a shower is wanted, it can be obtained at a truck stop along the road.

Campgrounds are often overcrowded, and reservations may sometimes be necessary in advance. Alternatively, particularly in National Parks and Forests, spots are limited and are doled out on a first-come, first-serve basis. Whatever the basis, especially in popular areas at the height of the season, it is important to find out the situation in advance and to plan appropriately. For example, on a tour of Maine, reservations should be made at Baxter State Park, where they will guarantee a place, but one should plan to get to Acadia National Park very early in order to get a campsite, after which one could make day tours around the Park.

Saving Money on the Road

If cost is an important consideration on the trip, it should be included in the planning stage. Supplies are much less expensive if they are bought at larger shopping centers rather than small country stores. Staples will be much cheaper if they are bought in larger quantities. Obviously, taking advantage of these savings will sometimes require that larger loads be carried for greater distances.

By the same token, avoiding expensive campgrounds will sometimes require riding farther or sleeping in a field by the side of the road. The more remote the area, the less problem there is likely to be in finding a free campsite.

With a little care, bicycle camping can be very inexpensive, since one can usually find somewhere to camp free, and one is left with only food and fuel to buy.

A Few Kinds of Trips

The most common pattern for a bicycle camping trip is a circuit, leaving from home, car, or public transportation. Sojourns from one point to another can be arranged by judicious use of buses, planes, or trains—or cars can be exchanged by two parties travelling in opposite directions. With the exchange method, it is usually best to drive the other party's car to your starting point so that the problems of finishing at different times and exchanging cars don't have to be faced at the end of a long day.

A lot of very interesting trips can be planned combining the use of bicycles and ferries. Boats can be included as one leg of a number of circuit trips around the Great Lakes and along the East Coast. There are also many islands which are served by ferries, and they often have fine campsites and make wonderful tours. The coastal ferries which serve the ports of northern British Columbia and Alaska could be readily used as part of many longer bicycle camping trips, and for cyclists going to Alaska they provide a scenic method of bypassing most of the gravel section of the Alaska Highway, which has too much truck traffic and dust to be very good for cycling.

Very interesting circuit trips can also be devised combining the use of bicycles with other kinds of non-motorized camping—backpacking, canoeing, or even ski touring. The bicycle can be left at one side of a mountain range, for example, and then a backpacking trip beginning at the other side brings one to the bicycle. This way the trip can be ended with a pleasant bike tour back to the car. The bike can also be left at the end of a long downriver canoe or kayak run so it can be used in riding back to get the automobile. One can even use the bicycle as transportation to the trailhead on mountaineering trips. The possibilities for such combined tours are limited only by the imagination.

APPENDICES

Appendix I—ADDITIONAL READING

A good repair manual is very useful for the bicycle camper, not to carry along in his panniers, but to use in maintaining his bike and learning about it. The author's personal favorite is *Anybody's Bike Book*, written by Tom Cuthbertson who has a wit that comes through even in a repair manual, and published by the Ten Speed Press in Berkeley. There are a number of other good repair books. *Derailleur Bicycle Repair* is excellent, published by Crown. *Richard's Bicycle Book* by Richard Ballantine is published by Ballantine, Stephen Henckel's *Bikes, A How-to-do-it Guide* by Chatham, and John Mc-Farlane's *It's Easy to Fix Your Bicycle* by Follett. *Glenn's Complete Bicycle Manual* by Clarence Coles and Harold Glenn (Crown) devotes most of its space to bikes of no interest to the touring cyclist, but it does have some useful information not covered elsewhere on subjects like overhauling feeewheels. Finally, a number of the general books mentioned below have some repair information.

The Complete Book of Bicycling by Eugene Sloane is the best general book on bicycling that has been written for an American audience, and it is a gold mine of useful information. The sections recommending particular bikes are out-of-date, however. Tom Cuthbertson's *Bike Tripping* is more fun than any other general book, and the section on frames (written by master frame builder Al Eisentraut) should be read by anyone interested in the technical aspects of this subject. Some other titles of interest are: Reginald Shaw's *Cycling*, published by Teach Yourself Books in London; *The Gold Medal Bicycle Handbook*, written by John Savage and published by Fawcett; *Bicycling, A Golden Guide* by George Fichter and Keith Kingsley (Golden); *The Clear Creek Bike Book* published by Signet. Two Wheel Travel's *Bicycle Camping and Touring* has some good material, and for general inspirational material, *The Best of Bicycling!*, edited by Harley Leete and published by Trident, is a pleasant potpourri of two-wheel tales.

There are now three bicycling magazines being published in the U.S. for the general cycling audience, so the long dry period that heretofore prevailed may finally come to an end. The oldest, which is getting better, is *Bicycling!*, available at $8 per year from P.O. Box 3330, San Rafael, California 94901. *Bicycle Spokesman* costs $8 a year, and can be had from Hub Circulation Co., 119 E. Palatine Road, Palatine, Illinois. *Bike World*, which is currently the best of the lot, is $3 per year, but will go to $7 when it goes to monthly publication. The address is P.O. Box 366, Mountain View, California 94040.

Various cycling magazines are published abroad. Probably one of the most interesting is *Cycletouring*, the publication of the Cyclists' Touring Club, which one can get either by joining the club or by subscribing. The price is $2.80 or an international money order for £1. The address is the Cyclists' Touring Club National Headquarters, 69 Meadrow Godalming, Surrey, England.

Those looking for suggested tours can go to several sources. Looking through back issues of cycling magazines is one good way to get ideas. The *North American Bicycle Atlas*, edited by Warren Asa and put out by the American Youth Hostels, is a nice compilation of tours. Joining the League of American Wheelmen will put one in contact with a great source of practical experience. Compilations of tours are now coming off the presses at a furious rate, and many more will no doubt be available by the time this book is published, so the reader would do well to write the publishers of those listed here for up-to-date information. Touchstone Press, P.O. Box 81, Beaverton, Oregon 97005, has already published *55 Oregon Bike Trips* by the Janowskis and *50 Northern California Bike Trips* by

Tom Murphy. Ten Speed Press, 2510 Bancroft Way, Berkeley, California 94704, besides publishing the two excellent books by Tom Cuthbertson, has also brought out *JJ's Best Bike Trips* by Joanne Johnston, whose best bike tours are in Northern California. KM Enterprises, Box 5568, Los Angeles, California 90055 has produced *Bicycle Trails of Southern California*. Finally, Gousha Publications, 2001 The Alameda, San Jose, California 95150, is the publisher of Marian May's *California Bike Tours* and of the seemingly unlikely *Bicentennial Bike Tours,* a collection of tours germane to the history and spirit of the founding of the United States.

The atlas mentioned for climatic information and some other useful data as well is *The National Atlas of the United States of America,* which was compiled by the Geological Survey of the Department of the Interior and is available from the Government Printing Office.

Probably the best general camping book available is Paul Cardwell's *America's Camping Book* (Scribner's). Books on backpacking are generally more in tune with the needs of the cyclist, because backpackers also have to watch their weight. The author's *America's Backpacking Book* is published by Scribner's. *The Complete Walker* by Colin Fletcher (Macmillan) is delightful. A third point of view is provided by Harvey Manning in *Backpacking, One Step At A Time* (Random House). Also, there's a lot of good information in Robert Colwell's *Introduction to Backpacking,* published by Stackpole Books.

Those interested in making their own equipment would be well advised to pick up a copy of Gerry Cunningham and Margaret Hansson's *Light Weight Camping Equipment and How To Make It* and to read it through twice.

Appendix II—
WHERE TO GET IT

The suppliers listed here all provide mail-order service, and nearly all of them have catalogues. Unfortunately, most bicycle mail-order houses charge a dollar or two for them. Occasionally, this is refundable with the first order. Camping suppliers generally send their literature free. The list here is fairly complete for businesses specializing in bicycle mail orders and providing catalogues. The camping suppliers are selected, either for their completeness or because they have unique products. The order is alphabetical.

ACTION ACCESSORIES, Box 15, Liverpool, New York 13088
    Catalogue $1, refundable with $5 order.

THE ALTERNATIVE, 1275 Pleasant Street, Boulder, Colorado 80302
    Source for lightweight foldable clincher tires (cheaters).

L.L. BEAN, Freeport, Maine 04032
    Camping equipment and accessories, mainly in the older New England tradition. Free catalogue.

BIG WHEEL LIMITED, 340 Holly Street, Denver, Colorado 80220
    $2.10 for catalogue-handbook of bicycles and accessories.

BIKE TOURING CENTER, 22 Main Street, Middlebury, Vermont 05767
> Bikes and touring equipment. Free catalogue.

BISHOP'S ULTIMATE OUTDOOR EQUIPMENT, 6804 Millwood Road, Bethesda, Maryland 20034
> Free catalogue of tents.

BLACK'S, Ogdensburg, New York 13669
> British and other European camping equipment. Free catalogue.

BOOKS ABOUT BICYCLING, P.O. Box 208b, Nevada City, California 95959
> An 8c stamp will bring a catalogue of the books listed here and many others.

CAMP AND TRAIL OUTFITTERS, 21 Park Place, New York, New York 10007
> Free catalogue with a good selection of camping equipment.

EASTERN MOUNTAIN SPORTS, 1041 Commonwealth Avenue, Boston, Massachusetts 02215
> One of the most complete catalogues of camping gear, including some kits.

EUR INTERNATIONAL, P.O. Box 45, Dayton, Ohio 45406
> Catalogue of bicycle items for $2.

FROSTLINE, P.O. Box 9100, Boulder, Colorado 80302
> Makers of kits for lightweight camping equipment, panniers, and handlebar bags. Free catalogue.

HIGHLAND OUTFITTERS, P.O. Box 121, Riverside, California 92502
> Free catalogue of lightweight camping gear.

HOLUBAR, Box 7, Boulder, Colorado 80302
> Makers of lightweight camping equipment, including Carikit kits. Free catalogue.

KELTY, 1801 Victory Boulevard, Glendale, California 91201
> Packs and other lightweight camping equipment. Free catalogue.

MOOR AND MOUNTAIN, Main Street, Concord, Massachusetts 01742
> A nice selection of lightweight camping gear, somewhat different

than most suppliers, including one large, lightweight open-front tent. Free catalogue.

MOUNTAIN SAFETY RESEARCH, 631 South 96th Street, Seattle, Washington 98108
Generally specializing in mountain climbing gear, they make the best thought-out stove and excellent tents, polyester-filled sleeping bags, etc. Free catalogue.

NORTH FACE, 1234 Fifth Street, Berkeley, California 94710
High quality lightweight camping equipment. Free catalogue.

OPEN AIR BICYCLES, 28 W. Cabrillo Boulevard, Santa Barbara, California 93101
Suppliers of the very well-designed Kangaroo panniers.

PLEASANT VALLEY SHOPPE, P.O. Box 293, Livingston, New Jersey 07039
25c brings brochure on tires and other items.

GENE PORTUESI, 6447 Michigan Avenue, Detroit, Michigan 48210
His Cycle-Pedia catalogue-handbook goes for $2.

RECREATIONAL EQUIPMENT, 1525 - 11th Avenue, Seattle, Washington 98122
One of the largest and least expensive suppliers of lightweight camping gear in the country. It is a cooperative; $1 membership entitles one to catalogues and to a partial rebate on purchases at the end of the year. They have started to carry bike panniers and packs, but these are not yet as well thought out as they should be.

SIERRA DESIGNS, 4th and Addison Streets, Berkeley, California 94710
Manufacturer and supplier of fine quality lightweight camping equipment. Free catalogue.

SINK'S BICYCLE WORLD, 816 South Washington Street, Marion, Indiana 46952
Catalogue of cycling equipment for $1.

SKI HUT, 1615 University Avenue, Berkeley, California 94703
One of the largest suppliers and manufacturers of quality lightweight equipment for camping. Carries Bellweather bike packs. Free catalogue.

STEPHENSON'S, 23206 Hatteras Street, Woodland Hills, California 91364

Makers of very lightweight, excellent, and expensive tents, sleeping bags, etc. Free catalogue.

TOURING CYCLIST SHOP, P.O. Box 4009, Boulder, Colorado 80302

Makers of the best (and most expensive) panniers available. They also supply chamois crotches and various other items of interest to tourers. Free brochures.

UNITED STATES GEOLOGICAL SURVEY

For maps of areas east of the Mississippi River write to Distribution Section, U.S.G.S., 1200 South Eads St., Arlington, Va. 22202; for maps of areas west of the Mississippi River write to Distribution Section, U.S.G.S., Federal Center, Denver, Colorado 80225. State index maps (with price lists) free. *Note:* While these are the chief sources for standard topographic maps of the U.S., some of these maps are often also sold by various stores such as sporting goods stores, supply stores near popular vacation areas, etc. Anticipate map needs as far ahead of time as possible; when expecting to obtain them through the Distribution Sections it may take two to three weeks to obtain the desired state index and another three to four weeks to secure the desired map(s). When maps are out of print temporarily, waiting time can drag into months.

VELOCIPEDE, 611 East Pine, Seattle, Washington 98122

Catalogue-handbook of bicycles and equipment is $2.

WALT'S BIKE SHOP, 1203 Rogers, Columbia, Missouri 65201

50c for catalogue of bicycle accessories.

WARE'S CYCLES, 2656 North 76th Street, Milwaukee, Wisconsin 53213

$2 for bike and accessory catalogue.

WEST RIDGE, 11930 West Olympic Boulevard, West Los Angeles, California

Free catalogue of lightweight camping equipment.

WHEEL GOODS, 2737 Hennepin, Minneapolis, Minnesota 55408

$2 for their large handbook-catalogue of bicycles and associated items.

Appendix III—
ORGANIZATIONS

Local bicycle clubs are one of the best sources of information and inspiration. They range from informal groups of enthusiasts who just go out and ride together once a week to large organizations with many scheduled trips and activities. The Bicycle Institute of America, 122 East 42nd Street, New York, New York 10017, is a trade association which puts out a lot of useful information. They will send a copy of *Bicycle Clubs Directory and Other Stuff* free for the asking. It has a listing of clubs, touring groups, and the like, along with other useful information. A list of clubs can also be found in the May, 1973, issue of *Bicycling!* magazine and probably will appear annually in revised form. One can also just drop by a local cycle shop and ask about clubs.

Several national groups deserve special mention here. The League of American Wheelmen is an ancient and venerable association that dates from the original American bicycle craze of the 19th century. It went defunct with the rise of the automobile, but it is now revived and kicking. It now serves as one of the most effective public advocates of cyclists' interests and can be a great help to anyone planning a tour. Membership includes a directory of members and a monthly publication. Write them at 5118 Foster Avenue, Chicago, Illinois 60630.

Those interested in spending some nights at hostels will want to join the A.Y.H. Write them and look over the list of hostels and the rules to see if they fit your conception of the trip. A.Y.H. cards are also accepted in thousands of hostels abroad. The address is American Youth Hostels, Inc., 20 West 17th Street, New York, New York 10011.

INDEX

air mattresses   55-57
altitude   43-44, 171-72
American Youth Hostels   15,
    188
ankling   148
axes   60-61

backpacking
    combining with bike
        tours   17-18, 179
    comparison with bike
        touring   16-17
backpacks for bike touring
    128, 135-36
    improvised   135-36
bicycle camping
    and backpacking   14-16
    and car camping   14-16
    and European-style
        touring   14-16, 22
    basics   23-24

combined with other light-
    weight travel   17-18, 179
getting started   18-21
in cold weather   82-83
in the desert   84-85
in the mountains   81-82
in wet weather   85
bicycles   86-127
    bearings   106, 118
    brakes   109,110, 112
    breaking in   87
    carriers   20, 130-32; for
      children   138, 144
    chains   95, 119
    cleats   114-16, 162
    cranks   104-05, 118, 121
    fenders   112
    frames   88-93
    freewheels   96, 118, 121,
      122, 123, 176-77
    front bags   130, 134;
        pattern   138-143

bicycles, continued

gears   93-99, 159
handlebars   111-112, 147-48
hubs   106-08, 118, 121
judging quality   87-91
lights   57, 112-14, 165-67
loading   128-144
locking   20, 116-17
packs   130, 133-36, 138-143
panniers   130, 133-35; front 131; patterns 138-143
pedals   106
pumps   114
rain covers   114
repairs   117-123, 176-77
rims   108
saddles   110-11
shoes   114-16
size   91-93
spare parts and tools   118-123, 176-77
spokes   107, 118, 120, 121, 122-24, 176
stem extension   111-12
tires and tubes   99-103, 121, 164, 177
transporting   123-27
trailers   144
types for touring   18-20, 86-87
wheels   106-08
books for additional reading   89, 180-82
brakes   109-110, 112, 121
breakfast   44

cadence   146-47
campgrounds, organized   27-28, 177-78
camping   22-61, 81-85
in cold weather   82-85
in the desert   84-85

camping, continued

in the mountains   81-82
in wet weather   85, 175
campsites   24-28, 84, 168-69, 177-78
canoeing combined with bike touring   17-18, 179
car camping compared with bike camping   16-17
carbide lamps   58-60
carriers   130-32
for children   138, 144
for mounting bike on car   123-27
purchase   20
chains   95, 119
security   20, 116-17
chamois seats for shorts and pants   49
clothing   48-51
for cold weather   82-83, 158-59, 161-63
gloves   148-49
in desert   163-64
rainwear   50-54, 85, 157-59
shoes   114-16
visibility   151, 166
cold weather   31
batteries in   58
camping in   82-83
carbide lamps in   82-83
riding in   158-59, 161-63
compasses   174
cooking   32-48
at high altitude   43-44
one-pot meals   33-36
over a fire   32, 37-41, 176
over a stove   32, 33, 37-38, 41-43, 176
utensils   46-47

derailleurs   95-97, 98, 121-22
deserts   84-85, 163-64, 172
dirt roads   164-65, 171

distances, planning   21,
    170-74, 175
down   65, 67-69

equipment   23-24, 29-31, 41-43,
    46-80, 86-127, 130-144,
    164-166, 175-77
    what to buy first   18-20

ferries   179
fires   23-24, 25, 26, 27-41,
    176
    building   38-40
    permits   37
flashlights   57-60
foam pads   55-57, 83
food
    breakfasts   44
    lunches   44
    planning and purchase   17,
        32-33, 44, 175-76
    recipes   35-36
    salads   36
    soups   36-37
fuel   41-43, 83, 176

gear ratios   93-99, 159;
    charts   98-99
Globaline   45
Golden Eagle pass   28
ground beds   55-57, 83

Halazone   45
hands, numbness and prevention
    148-49
headlamps   57-60, 166-67
hills   21, 149-150, 159-161
hostels   14-16, 188

insects   27, 55, 61

knives   60

lights   57-60, 112-14, 165-67
locks   20, 116-17

lunches   44

magazines   181
maps   169-170, 172-175
millipore filters   46
mountains   81-82, 159-161

night riding   165-67

organizations for cyclists
    187-188

pace   21, 146-47, 170-72
panniers   130, 133-35
    front   131, 134
    patterns   138-143
patterns
    bike packs   138-143
    rainwear   52-54
pedalling speeds   146-47
pennants for visibility   151
planning   23-24, 168-179
    first trips   20-21
    food   32-33, 175
    water   45, 46, 163,
        175-176

rain   50-51, 52-54, 85, 156,
    157-59, 171, 173
reflective materials   166
renting equipment   20
reservations at campgrounds   27,
    169, 177-78
riding techniques   145-167

salt   43, 163
saws   60-61
shelters   28-31
shoes   114-116, 161-62
sleeping   51-55
sleeping bags   55, 62-71
stoves   23-24, 26, 32, 33,
    37-38, 41-43, 176
    lighting   41-43
sun protection   161, 163-64

suppliers   183-86

tarpaulins   29, 31, 78-79, 84
tents   27, 28-29, 62, 72-80, 85
    design   74-78
    flies   74, 75, 77
    floors   77
    for cold weather   83
    recommendations   29-31,
       78-70
    stakes   28, 30, 77, 78, 130
    tube   26-27, 29-31, 83
theft, bicycle   20, 116-17

tires   99-103, 121, 122, 164, 177
touring, European-style   14-16
traffic survival   150-54, 157,
    162-63
training   21, 145-48

water   25, 175-76
    carrying   45, 46
    in desert   84-85, 163-64
    purification   44-46
weight   17, 23, 24, 128-29, 144
wind   21, 81, 155-56, 171, 173
wind resistance   24